WHY PEOPLE FAIL

WHY PEOPLE FAIL

DR. HERBERT S. STREAN
WITH LUCY FREEMAN

WYNWOOD® PRESS
Tarrytown, New York

Library of Congress Cataloging-in-Publication Data

Strean, Herbert S.
Why people fail : breaking the cycle of self-defeating behavior / Herbert Strean with Lucy Freeman. — 1st ed.
p. cm.
ISBN 0-922066-76-0
1. Failure (Psychology). 2. Success—Psychological aspects.
I. Freeman, Lucy. II. Title.
BF575.F14S77 1992
158'.1—dc20 91-28672
CIP

Published by Wynwood® Press
Tarrytown, New York
An Imprint of Gleneida Publishing Group
Printed in the United States of America
First Edition

ACKNOWLEDGMENTS

First we wish to acknowledge our creative, energetic, and gracious editor, Patricia Kossmann, Executive Editor and Publisher of Wynwood Press. She has been a very helpful supporter and constructive adviser ever since we conceived the idea of this book.

We would also like to thank our literary agent, Jane Dystel, of Acton and Dystel, Inc., who believed in the value of our idea and helped us carry our thoughts on success and failure to fruition. She continues to impress us with her deep sensitivity as to what readers want and how they wish it to be presented.

We thank many of Dr. Strean's patients, who have been our major consultants. They have helped us become sensitized to the many dimensions of failure and have shown what is necessary to resolve failure and climb the ladder of success.

Finally, the authors are indebted to each other for the

successful completion of this book. Working on it together has helped us overcome some of our own failures and in turn enabled us to look at ourselves and each other as more successful.

The reader will probably be interested to know about our collaboration. Dr. Strean, the psychotherapist and teacher, furnished the major ideas on failure and the vignettes of patients. Lucy Freeman, author and editor, transformed this material into readable English.

Herbert S. Strean
Lucy Freeman

AUTHORS' NOTE

In order to insure confidentiality, all names of patients are pseudonyms, and all identifying data have been altered. Further, in most cases the patient is an amalgam of several individuals.

CONTENTS

INTRODUCTION

Failure needs no introduction. Not one human being is exempt from failure. Throughout our lives we set goals and find we cannot possibly achieve every one of them.

Our failures start early. As toddlers we strive for the goal of walking but often fall. When we enter kindergarten we are supposed to be toilet-trained but suffer accidents. In first grade we may not be able to master reading, writing, and arithmetic and our teacher gives us an *F*. Failure is such an ever-present phenomenon in the halls of learning that *F* is no mystery to anyone from the first grade to a Ph.D. program.

Our journey through life contains many failures. Adolescents often become depressed when they fail in romantic relationships, competitive sports, or sexual adventures. As adults we experience marriages, businesses, and friends and relatives that somehow fail us. As senior citizens our memories fail us, words fail us, and as we near the end of life's journey our health, too, fails us.

Failures may be both large and small. We can fail to dial the correct phone number and not feel too upset. Or we can be outraged, then depressed, when we fail in love, learning, or business. Failing is never pleasant; it can be slightly irritating or deeply devastating. Some who have failed in love, marriage, or work become disillusioned with their partners, outraged, and unable to sleep.

Many of us, perhaps most of us, make immediate excuses for our failures. There is a term we often use as we hear the other fellow rationalize his failures—*sour grapes.* We haul it out when we do not wish to feel the pain of failure. We may say, to justify ourselves, "I didn't want the crummy job anyhow." Or "He wouldn't have been a good mate, he's too wrapped up in himself." Or "Who wants to be the victim of the backbreaking post?" after we have lost the election.

One of the fascinating dimensions of failure is that each one of us reacts to it in our own idiosyncratic manner. One man during a 1991 recession lost his job as a sanitation worker in Manhattan and jumped off a roof, leaving a wife and three children. Another, who lost the identical job at the same time, smiled broadly and said, "What a relief to get rid of that boring work! I'm going to find something more rewarding."

We have often seen men and women respond to the same event very differently, so that at times it seems difficult to define or even understand what constitutes failure. When we feel disappointed, we may react from outrage and depression on one end of the scale to indifference and relief on the other. Some college students are pleased to hear they have flunked out; others become extremely dejected, even suicidal.

Perhaps one of the best examples of how differently individuals respond to failure is noted in the military. The designation 4-F means the young man has failed to meet the physical requirements of the army. On receiving the 4-F evaluation, some men have been extremely gleeful whereas others become intensely morose.

We can react to the same failure in a very different manner from one day to the next. Perhaps we feel in an expansive mood when we lose a few dollars at a poker game, even laugh and say, "It was such fun playing, the loss was worth it." But if the next time we play we feel irritable and tired and we lose a few dollars, we may curse loudly, feeling angry both at ourselves and at the winners.

Many of us respond to rejections and other slights very differently, depending on what is taking place in our inner lives. If we enjoyed a good night's sleep and someone hugged us warmly as we left home in the morning, a colleague's grimace will not seriously affect our mood. However, we may call ourselves worthless failures a week later, when the same colleague gives us the same grimace, if we are not feeling in the expansive and self-confident mood we felt seven days before.

Failure has many faces, many causes, and many forms. While Webster's dictionary defines *failure* as "the inability to achieve a goal," this definition does not reveal the many complexities, the many subtleties, the many causes of failure. Obviously no dictionary can supply us with the answers to How do I overcome failure?

Our aim is to help the reader understand why he fails at a task at which he consciously desires to succeed. We hope to help him turn disaster into success and become a winner.

This is eminently possible if we understand our role in our own failures and stop ascribing those failures to outside events, to chance, and to other people who are out to hurt us. One of the best ways to recognize a chronic failure is that person's constant complaint that external forces and other men and women are conspiring to create injustices in his life over which he has no control.

On the other hand, a successful person is one who takes responsibility for himself, recognizes both his own strengths and his own limitations. He also rarely views himself as a victim of circumstance. He accepts that neither he nor anyone else can be perfect and win all the battles waged.

We will differentiate between objective failure and subjective failure. By *objective* failure we refer to the *actual* events that take place and comprise a "failure"—not achieving enough points on an examination, going bankrupt, seeking a divorce, or experiencing the end of a love relationship.

All of these objective events, which are clear to others as well as to ourselves, induce *subjective* reactions—our emotional, nonrational responses to failure based on earlier experiences in our life. These responses may become so intense that for the moment we believe they are too devastating to bear. On the opposite end of the scale of feelings, a marriage can fail but the husband or wife feels happy, relieved to say goodbye to a torturous relationship. Different individuals respond in their own unique, subjective manner.

All of us have met men and women we would certainly call successful even though they might regard themselves as failures. A multimillionaire, using society's standards, would be called a success. But subjectively this man's ideals and goals may be such that he considers himself a failure. In our society certain vocations have limited—even negative—status. No doubt many believe that people in these positions have failed to achieve their potential, even though they seem content, at home with the tasks that are part of their work.

We have all met attractive-looking men and women whom we envy and consider eminently successful, only to find they disparage themselves. On the other hand, we have met individuals whom we disparage or demean, yet they consider themselves happy and successful.

Many a child or teenager can respond to a grade of *B*+ or *A*− with dejection and feel like a failure, while others can receive a *C* or *C*+ and jump for joy. The latter are more than satisfied to be average, and can like themselves without being outstanding. We will return to this theme many times during the course of this book.

Failure from a psychological perspective is therefore difficult to define. Any definition of failure must consider exactly what a person is setting out to achieve. If he has a goal of eternal bliss, where life is constantly ecstatic, then he will feel like a failure 99 percent of the time. On the other hand, if he contends that life is far from a bowl of cherries, that misfortunes and injustices abound, then a few hours of relaxation may make his day feel serene and successful.

We can make our lives more enjoyable and successful if we set realistic goals for ourselves and for those with whom we work and live. If we believe our marriages should be consistently joyful twenty-four hours a day, seven days a week, that our mate should love us consistently and constantly, that our home should be a place where "never is heard a discouraging word," then we will feel miserable in marriage, and the relationship will be in danger of terminating.

On the other hand, if we recognize that every mate in the world, including ourselves, has limitations and vulnerabilities and that this piece of reality is not a cause for doom or alarm, then we will feel more loving, less hateful, and we will experience greater pleasure, less pain.

If we must write the great American novel or achieve eternal fame in some way, we are apt to be failures. In other words, if we set grandiose expectations for ourselves, we will constantly be disappointed and feel like failures. Or if we expect those close to us constantly to reinforce, love, and admire us, we feel they fail us if they dare disagree.

Subjective happiness evolves when we see life as it is, not as we demand that it be. Children can achieve high marks if they do not feel pressured constantly by parents to "be first" and "get all *A*s." Whether the ballplayer is a child, a teenager, or an adult, his batting average is apt to be much higher if he does not feel he must hit a home run every time. Successful actors and actresses who have done well on Broadway have pointed out that success started when they failed to be chosen after an audition and did not feel this was the end of their career.

One of the keys to resolving failures is to understand better how and why we experience them as we do. Many of us view our inability to achieve in love, work, or play as a severe stigma. We berate ourselves because we believe we must be the best and the most beautiful or the most handsome in order to feel successful, despite the fact that no person can ever attain all the achievements he fantasizes, be they in work, love, or elsewhere.

Our major message in this book is that we ourselves have arranged most of the failures we experience. Most failures can be overcome if we recognize how and why we somehow produced them, for failure in most instances is a script written unconsciously by the one who fails. We might well ask why so many persons arrange their own failures.

For one thing, many of us feel that when we succeed in work, play, or relationships we are frauds; we believe our success is not justified. Anyone who practices psychotherapy or counsels people who have difficulty coping with life, hears the following sentiment several times a day: "I have to work hard to enjoy my success. If I haven't worked hard and slaved away, then I'm not entitled to success."

I have heard this remark from businessmen who made lucrative deals, writers who have written books that sold extremely well, and men and women who are loved unconditionally by attractive partners but feel they do not deserve success in these areas.

One of the limitations of living in a society dominated by the Protestant work ethic is that we tend to feel unworthy of our success unless we have paid a heavy price and suffered immeasurably. If someone loves us without our having done something outstanding for that person, we tend to devalue that love.

As Groucho Marx once said, "I would never join a country club that wanted me as a member."

Another major reason why we arrange to fail in so many of our pursuits is that most of us falsely believe that if we are successful, superior, and stand out from lesser souls, we make others suffer. As our examples from everyday life will demonstrate, because we all competed with siblings and with our parents, particularly the parent of the same gender, there is a tendency to feel that when we are successful we face an alienated family and friends.

When we are successful, friends and family may very well be envious and angry. But if we take their resentments too seriously, feel bereft because they cannot applaud us, then we agree with them that we are maliciously out to hurt them. The successful person has to learn to handle humbly the envy of others. You cannot be successful and not be envied by friend or foe. You cannot be a real winner without trying to cope with the anger and castigation of the losers who surround you.

One of the major reasons for writing about failure and success is to show men and women that if they can learn to accept the envy and resentment of those who cannot tolerate the successes of anyone else, success will be much more assured. We like ourselves more as we cease trying to appease those we are close to, stop trying to win the love of those who resent us for being successful.

Many of us tend to view success as if we are the receiver of stolen goods. All too often we think we have seized the much-wanted job, the much-desired lover, the much-coveted possession, the much-wanted vacation abroad, from someone near and dear, making that person our foe. Too often failure is self-imposed because we feel guilty about success. We cannot tolerate our success, so we arrange, albeit unconsciously, to plunge into depression, to feel dejected or devalued in spite of our achievements.

I recall a businessman who worked an entire year to consummate a major deal. Two days after he received a substantial amount of money, he lost the check. As this man, my patient in therapy, explored with me what he felt, it became clear he had to punish himself for his achievement, feeling he was a dishonest tycoon who manipulated others.

Another major factor in failure is that once we have achieved something, we feel pressured to go on achieving more and more. Youngsters playing baseball often feel pressured to turn singles and doubles into home runs, and many students feel compelled to change *B*s into *A*s.

Very closely linked to arranging failure is our personal

history with our parents. Many of us are brought up to believe we will be loved only if we produce. This manipulation by parents induces rage in the child, which he buries to keep their love. Consequently, many resent having to prove themselves constantly to parental figures. Often academic, work-related, and other failures may be due to our strong wish to defy compulsive parents.

In all of us there still lives a child. To overcome failure we should learn to know this child as well as possible. For if we do not realize that the child within us often tries to spite his parents by still failing, or that the child within feels guilty because he has not worked hard enough or his progress has hurt a brother or sister, then we are not able to rewrite our failing scripts. We will continue to feel that the good life is passing us by.

As we discuss how to resolve failure, we will refer frequently to the tasks all of us face at each stage of our development—what writer Gail Sheehy referred to as passages, and what psychoanalyst Erik Erikson described as developmental tasks.

In order to feel successful, we need to have some degree of tender love and care from a mothering person. If we do not receive these important emotional ingredients, we will fail to trust others and ourselves. If we are not appropriately weaned, toilet-trained, and taught to accept a number of No's, we will fail to cope with life's uncertainties, limitations, and disappointments. We will continually yearn for an all-giving breast, to gratify ourselves instantly.

Growing up and maturing requires us to give up certain fantasies. If we insist, for instance, on acting like a prince or princess, we are bound to fail or feel like a failure. The boy who believes he has the right to be his mother's prince will later, as an adult, be disappointed in love, for no partner can gratify a mortal who wishes to act like an imaginary, selfish king of the realm.

If a girl aspires to be her father's favorite, she too will later find love relationships fraught with failure and misery. No adult man wants to be a father twenty-four hours a day when he lives with a woman.

As we go through life, we should keep in mind that being a passenger on that journey often requires accepting frustration, learning how to cooperate and empathize with others. Adolescence and young adulthood should afford us the opportunities to learn how to cope with grim realities.

One of the important issues we will discuss in depth is that almost all sexual failures are self-inflicted and self-arranged because the man or woman engaged in unenjoyable lovemaking distorts the partner and distorts himself. Making successful love requires a tolerance not only of the child within us but of the child within the partner. It also requires empathy and understanding as well as the capacity to regress without feeling overwhelmed.

We will show the reader that many failures are due to unresolved completion of early developmental tasks, which prevents any moving through later passages. We will describe how failures in love, work, marriage, and business can be resolved if people take time to understand how they have arranged the failures and what they can do to alter them.

We live in a society replete with all kinds of failures. Homicides and suicides have increased tenfold in the last five years. The drug culture is proliferating. Thousands of teenagers are alcoholics, severely depressed and miserable. Men and women are reportedly less happy in the workplace, and while there is more time for leisure, people are much less relaxed.

The habit of popping pills and taking all kinds of medication to ease anxiety is widespread. Increases in child abuse, sex abuse, and murder suggest that the seeds of hatred and violence lie everywhere. Our society is far from successful in helping men and women form a culture based on love, not hate.

Since none of us can really feel a success if we continually hold hatred in our hearts, we need to learn how this hatred can be understood and diminished so that love and caring may reign. We hope this book will help men, women, and children become both objective and subjective successes. This will not only offer them far happier lives but will lead to a more peaceful society.

CHAPTER 1

THE SECRET WISH TO FAIL

One spring day Beth, an attractive thirty-five-year-old woman, walked into my office just off Central Park West and 96th Street in Manhattan. She had called previously to ask for a consultation.*

She sat down slowly in the chair opposite mine, sighed, then spoke in a well-modulated voice, choosing her words carefully.

"I sought you out, Dr. Strean, because I seem to be going from one failure to another," she explained, a dejected expression on her face. "It seems to have affected my husband, too. I'm not sure he loves me any longer. Luckily, we don't have children."

Sighing again, she continued, "Once I was a top student in English and journalism at Oberlin College and longed to be editor of one of New York's largest magazines. When

* Names of all patients are pseudonyms.

I graduated I took a job as secretary at *Vanity Fair,* hoping eventually to have the necessary experience to fulfill my lifelong goal."

Beth told me how, after eight years of perseverance, struggle, and hard work she had advanced from secretary to office manager to copy editor. She finally achieved the status of senior editor in a major division of a well-known national magazine.

Following an initial feeling of elation, she recalled she started to behave far differently than when she was an office manager and copy editor. She said, "I don't know what happened but when I became boss I started to argue vehemently with my superiors. I turned very critical and became involved in all kinds of power struggles."

She added, "I arrived late for appointments, started to feel nauseous every day, became an insomniac and was depressed much of the time."

As I reflected silently about what she was saying, I was keenly aware of how differently Beth reacted at the time she was boss as opposed to when she was bossed. If someone else had control she was cooperative, pleasant, somewhat compliant, easy to live with, and easy to live with herself. But as boss, she was belligerent, critical, fought with everyone, and suffered deeply. After a year she was fired from the job she had so ardently desired.

She told me, "At first I was convinced everyone was out to get me, resented my status. But since the same thing happened two times after that at other magazines, I knew there must be something inside me that makes me a different person when I am a success."

"That's why I came to see you, Dr. Strean. I need help," she added sadly, a tear or two in her large blue eyes.

It took several sessions before Beth and I could begin to understand why a sensitive, creative, bright, vigorous woman, who did well in other areas of living, had become so inept and self-destructive after she achieved her lifelong ambition.

Fear of Success

What did Beth and I learn as we examined together her inability to succeed at something for which she so strongly yearned?

We discovered that she had to punish herself for getting what she wanted because she felt strong pangs of guilt when she achieved her fervent desire, as though she did not deserve success.

After a few months of weekly therapy with Beth, I told her it seemed quite clear she was punishing herself for achieving what she wanted so intensely.

I asked, "What comes to mind about being an editor that makes you convinced that punishment and misery, rather than pleasure and comfort, are your just, or rather unjust, rewards?"

Beth was quiet a few moments, then said slowly, "I believe I am not entitled to this wonderful job of being an editor." She added, "I know it sounds crazy but I feel as though I am taking the job away from others who deserve it more."

For the first time in our work together tears streamed down her face. She took out a handkerchief, wiped them away. With much anguish, as if confessing to the crime of murder, she said, "I feel very greedy. As if I want too much and take too much—all of it. My husband threatens to leave because he says he no longer finds me lovable. He says my work comes before anything else and he doesn't want such a wife."

She fell silent, staring at the floor.

"Why do you feel so greedy about your work?" I asked.

She said slowly, as though figuring out the answer, "The only time I ever felt greedy was when I was ten and my brother Tony was five. We both dashed for the piece of apple pie we knew was left in the refrigerator after dinner. Since I was the oldest I felt I was entitled to it. I grabbed it and quickly devoured it without offering him a bite."

She bit her lips, then went on, "It was a very selfish thing to do and I hated myself. My father and mother rushed in when they heard Tony wail, 'That's not fair!' and my father said sternly, 'You're a mean sister!' Since my parents were always right, I knew I deserved his condemnation. I *had* been selfish and mean."

She stopped again, then told me, "I felt the same way at Oberlin when I was chosen valedictorian of the graduating class. I knew the other students wanted to be in my place. I felt I had stolen something precious from them. I heard my parents shouting at me, 'You mean sister!' I had stolen the honor from my classmates much like I stole the apple pie from my brother Tony."

Beth then reported other examples from the past and present where she turned successful triumphs into disastrous defeats. Each time she felt she achieved something she possessed the strong feeling she was a mean sister. In her mind any achievement turned into a hostile crime, as if she took all the pleasure for herself and deprived others of their rights—their emotional or literal piece of pie. Because she was so mean she believed that her parents, her brother Tony, and the whole world, including her husband, no longer loved her, and she felt deeply depressed.

As I listened to Beth castigate, berate, and demean herself, I thought of an old Chinese saying, "If greed were a fever, all the world would be dead." Everyone is somewhat greedy at times, especially when it comes to food.

Why did I think of this Chinese adage, I asked myself. I recalled it because I was keenly aware of the fact that Beth, like millions of other men and women, tended to equate her success with theft and greed (millionaires give thousands of dollars to charities to ease their conscience). This is a serious distortion of the meaning of success, yet it was what Beth, like the millionaires, felt deeply in her heart and prevented her from achieving her goal in life.

What made Beth feel so greedy when she reached the top executive position on the magazine? When adults aspire to something they deem desirable and precious, as the editorship was to Beth, they have a strong tendency to feel like a child once again. When we want something avariciously it is inevitable that the child within, who never completely leaves us, becomes very much alive once again and may control us, causing us to feel guilty over unseemly behavior.

To Beth, the editorship was vital to her existence, just as a home run can be to a baseball player or a special sale can be to a salesman. The wish to be an editor dominated her thoughts; she felt much like the child who *must* have that delicious ice cream, that coveted toy, or that much-desired dress or pair of trousers. When the child in any of us emerges, we relive all the old competitions in which we insisted on being Number One. But then, as the adult in us takes over, we are drowned in guilt.

Just as Beth wished to take away the pie from her brother, so too did the child residing in her regard being an editor as a delicious piece of pie she did not wish anyone else to possess. Psychologically speaking, achieving the editor's position was to Beth stealing apple pie from her younger brother. She felt so guilty for her imaginary crime that she had to create situations where parental figures would punish her and make her into a bad girl all over again.

It was more than a coincidence that after Beth became an editor and felt like the thief who stole the pie, she felt nauseous so much of the time. She regressed in memory to the very moment she seized and devoured a piece of the pie she felt she should have shared with her brother. All of us tend to react like Beth when we achieve something precious to us but which appears forbidden.

The Meaning of Achievement

Realistically, there is nothing forbidden about most things we achieve, but the frightened child within distorts actual achievements, turning them into thefts, even fantasized murders. By becoming an editor Beth did not hurt a soul, but in her heart she felt she destroyed a whole group of fragile persons with whom she worked. All of her colleagues, women and men, turned into her brother Tony, as she felt she had taken away what belonged to them—the chance to be at the top, to eat or at least share the last piece of pie. She heard her parents' angry voices once again flagellate her with the words, "You mean sister!"

Like so many of us who feel we must fail, Beth could not tell the difference between her powerful childish wishes for which she was criticized and for which she lost the love of her parents momentarily, and her adult deeds. She reacted as most of us do as she thought her wishes and fantasies had become forbidden acts. She could not accept her normal hungry, greedy, and competitive wishes as part of being human.

Instead of seeing herself as a thirty-five-year-old woman

entitled to her achievements, she thought of herself as an evil spider woman who overpowered those with whom she worked, as she had overpowered her brother. Beth did what most guilty achievers do—she beat up on herself emotionally because she thought she had snatched victory away from others she wanted to keep as friends.

It is difficult for most adults to acknowledge that part of us always remains a child who wants what we want when we want it, feels like grabbing impulsively whatever we wish at the moment without worrying about others. As we grow up we learn we must help and respect the wishes and needs of others, share with them. Thus when we achieve what we desire as adults, and those close to us do not, we may believe we are robbers.

To enjoy what we achieve we have to be able not only to acknowledge our childish wishes and fantasies, but also to realize they are not evil deeds. We may play out in our minds our fantasies, such as imagining we are Superman, but we should not equate fantasy with reality or we will feel defeated, as Beth did.

We can learn from Beth's agony why we unconsciously arrange to feel miserable after success. She exaggerated the importance of her achievement and the power attached to her new status. I helped her understand that her success in competing for a job did not make her the spider woman the child part of her once longed to be.

Many of us distort the meaning of our achievements and then feel unworthy of them. Sometimes we give such preeminence to the achievement that we become depressed or even suicidal. In my day-to-day work as a psychotherapist I constantly try to help people understand that a major obstacle to their deriving pleasure from success is that they seriously distort the importance of the achievement. Some turn success, such as reaching the top in any profession, making a large sale, or winning a loved one, into a major war where they believe they have conquered the enemy and remain the only victor enjoying the spoils. Then, feeling greedy as well as omnipotent, they punish themselves for childish fantasies that are harmless but can seem overpowering if they have not been faced in the light of reason.

I helped one man who was close to suicide after he was selected as dean at a large university. He blamed himself for destroying every professor who sought that high position. Only when he could recognize the grandiosity of his wishes and the intensity of his own competitive desires could he function comfortably in his rightful new position.

A young college student came to me for help because she suddenly could not swallow food. Her self-imposed torture was precipitated by receiving an *A* on a term paper. She had envisioned the paper as equivalent to a best-selling novel and felt guilty of destroying every aspiring writer in North America. That fantasy made her believe she should die.

I have learned that actors and actresses, as well as successful businessmen, share similar fantasies. They believe they are so powerful, so greedy, so threatening to others that they must suffer for their intense fantasies.

For Beth to become a magazine editor was like a dream come true, but a dream that proved to be a nightmare. It centered on her memory of snatching food from the mouth of her little brother, repeated in the snatching of the top position from her friends at the magazine. Her guilt from the original sin of starving her brother as she ate the prized apple pie was still overwhelming. She heard over and over the words of her father, "You're a mean sister!"

I told her, as I have told many others over the years who

punished themselves for their achievement, that they are not as powerful as they believe they are. I reassure them we can realistically be proud of our achievements if we do not ascribe so much power to ourselves. When we imagine ourselves as destructive Napoleons or murderous Hitlers, we then believe we have to be destroyed emotionally because we are not entitled to the pleasure of our achievements.

All too many of us feel as if we are generals killing enemies or evil children wiping out parents and siblings. (The small hatreds of childhood sometimes rise to remind us of our imperfect past.) We have not learned to accept the fact that we are all limited mortals, no matter how much we achieve.

One man in therapy had been a consistent failure in all his relationships with women. Handsome, bright, competent, and likeable, he constantly saw himself as all-powerful. Walking into his session one day, he said in a boasting tone, "Last night I could have gone to bed with Elizabeth Taylor."

"Really? How come?" I asked in genuine astonishment.

"Because I had an erection," he said proudly.

In his mind, an erection made him Don Juan, who could seduce the most beautiful woman in the world just by looking at her. My patient's arrogance not only alienated women but because he thought he could destroy all men and win all women, he constantly feared the revenge of men and his potency with women.

When we feel we deserve punishment, we await the axe that will descend on our head, as Beth did when she bettered her colleagues. We lose all of our self-confidence because of the strong guilt that reminds us of what we consider past sins.

We must realize that wishing, past and present, is never

criminal and that a fantasy is never a crime. Our daydreams cannot hurt anyone. But if we believe that our wishes are the same as deeds, the way the child within us thinks, then as adults we will at times imagine we are murderers who deserve only prison. Many men and women live in psychological prisons, believing they should be incarcerated for their deadly thoughts even though they only indulge in harmless fantasies and childish daydreams.

Beth worked actively to achieve success, but when she won it she felt depressed and agitated. Many of us never even try to reach our potential because we anticipate all kinds of punishment. Without realizing it, we squelch our aspirations and ambitions to avoid hearing voices that will berate us as mean, selfish, or cruel.

We convince ourselves that family and friends will despise and envy us if we are a success. We fear we will be socially isolated if we achieve more than those to whom we have been close over the years. But what we do not tell ourselves is that we feel an unreal guilt, a hangover from our childish selfish wishes. Instead, we accept the criticism of those who deride and demean us, then feel we deserve punishment.

Because we feel guilty for wanting to surpass our rivals of childhood, we take criticisms too much to heart and view our accomplishments as provocative acts that hurt others. This is why we feel vulnerable to attack and believe that those who tear us down are justified.

A Broadway actress told me she never allowed her brothers and sisters to know when she appeared in a play because "they are so jealous of me." She wanted her siblings to be envious but feared their disapproval because she was still competitive. She failed to understand that they were human beings too. Even if they attended her performance and tore her apart, she would survive if she were not so convinced she was destroying them by her successful performances.

What Is Survivor Guilt?

Psychologists use the term *survivor guilt* to describe the feeling that attaining the good things in life is equal to betraying family members who are not so successful. We distort our prowess, believe it occurs at the expense of those near and dear. Beth suffered in part from survivor guilt because she concluded, although erroneously, that she deprived her brother as she gained victories at his expense. Those burdened by survivor guilt placate their consciences by giving up desirable positions or achievements their parents and siblings never acquired.

In marital counseling I have met hundreds of husbands and wives unable to enjoy a mutually loving relationship because they feel too guilty about enjoying marriage more than their parents did. One such woman was Evelyn, whose mother destroyed her own marriage by throwing endless temper tantrums. Evelyn ended her marriage in the same fashion, continually picking fights with her husband. One father indulged in extramarital affairs; when his son grew up, he too became an adulterer.

All of us suffer to some extent from survivor guilt because we all have had, and still possess, fantasies of forsaking our parents and siblings and enjoying a better life free of their influence. If we achieve that better life in a happy marriage, in lovable children and work we enjoy, we may distort once again the meaning of success. Guilt will follow as we punish ourselves needlessly.

Another term used in discussing failure is *separation*

guilt. It embodies the fantasy that if we become strong and independent, those we leave behind will die. We believe they need our presence in order to survive, that without us they perish.

This distorted belief, like all untrue beliefs, emanates from childhood. As children, we saw our parents, grandparents, and older siblings as powerful. We felt as if our lives depended on them. We needed them to survive, and the thought that they would not made us feel abandoned.

Yet all children at times resent their elders for the physical and emotional power they possess. One of the fondest wishes of a child is to reverse roles with his parents. Children enjoy playing mothers and fathers, schoolteachers, doctors, and nurses. They want others to be the weak child as they fantasize themselves as the strong adult. Any child who has had a tonsillectomy wants to play doctor, take out other children's tonsils. One of the fantasies of a child is to become a strong, independent adult and make his parents dependent, helpless children to whom he gives the orders. Consequently, there is a tendency in all of us, when we separate from our families and are on our own, truly grown up, to believe those we have deserted now feel like the helpless child we once felt like when our parents were not present. Some parents compound this feeling by telling us how devastated they are without our presence, especially if we move miles away.

Every time we change a job, leave a relationship, say no to someone we love, we are inclined to feel separation guilt. Many men and women believe that to stand alone successfully, to possess their own special status and unique identity, is to abandon those who have been close, leaving them devastated.

A salesman, George, fell into a deep depression after each successful deal. In high school he cherished a strong desire to leave home and become rich, which meant deserting his frustrating and demanding mother and father. In the unconscious part of his mind that meant killing them. To feel separate, independent, and successful meant in his distorted way of looking at life to be the murderer of his parents. He punished himself for any achievement and as a result his income was small.

Many college dropouts were successful in high school. Sally, an attractive nineteen-year-old and a brilliant high school student, left college after her freshman year. On consulting me she exclaimed, "When I did well in high school I felt loved. But when I reached college and my parents were no longer present to praise me, I felt I was no longer loved by anyone."

Sally thought that being separated from her parents made her too powerful and hurt those she loved. Torturing herself, she flunked her courses. Many a child homesick at camp or elsewhere fails to enjoy himself as he visualizes his parents and siblings suffering in the heat of the city.

Young men and women, older men and women too, believe they can't win. To become separate and autonomous is to forsake others, to turn loved ones into the helpless, sad children they once felt themselves to be. They do not want to believe they have committed a like crime.

All of us tend to distort to some degree our independence and erroneously believe that if we are strong, we cause our parents and siblings deep unhappiness. We then feel we must pay the price for what we believe to be a crime. We punish ourselves by failing at college, losing a job, alienating a loved one, or mistreating a child.

Other failures are due to what psychologists refer to as emotional blackmail. This implies that a child or adult is loved only if he fulfills certain conditions, such as getting high grades or excelling in sports or the arts or in the financial market.

Spouses and friends frequently use emotional blackmail. A husband loves his wife only if she is always smiling, willing to carry out his every command. He withdraws love and support if she looks unhappy or expresses the slightest show of anger or displeasure. A wife may love her husband only if he is a breadwinner; if he fails to amass a fortune, she withholds her love.

When a child or adult senses that he is loved only under certain conditions, he feels furious and may retaliate by failure. The pressured child who must bring home *A*'s may suddenly arrange to receive *C*'s as a way of punishing his parents. The Little League ballplayer who believes that his parents will be furious if he does not hit home runs is almost sure to strike out. The marital partner loved only under certain conditions may rebel and refuse to cater to his spouse's whims.

Emotional blackmail was illustrated dramatically in the movie *The Loneliness of the Long-Distance Runner,* in which the main character was pressured by friends and family to win every race. After many successes he sensed he would continue to be loved only if he were a constant winner. To spite family and friends, in the most important race of the year, running far ahead of the pack, appearing to be a sure winner, he came to an abrupt halt fifty yards before the finish line. He allowed every other runner to pass him, as though thumbing his nose at family and friends and saying, "If you don't love me the way I want to be loved, I'll torture you and make you suffer!"

Many men and women fail because they would rather be spiteful than succeed and please others. To comply with another's wish for them to succeed fills them with rage. Many of the children and adults I have seen in psychotherapy, although bright and competent, work hard to defeat me as they discharge hatred toward a parental figure. One young man, David, a college dropout, told me, "To cooperate with you makes me feel demeaned and exploited."

Many a bright child cannot read or write, add or subtract, because in one way or another he or she is sneering at parents, teachers, and the world, "I know you want me to learn and do well in school and it's because I'm aware you don't really love me for myself that I will do just the opposite to spite you."

Some children are so eager to defy parents and the adult world for loving them only if they produce what the parents want that I found I could help many through what is called negative suggestion. I have told several spiteful youngsters during therapy, "Maybe you'll be better off if you don't read or write, add or subtract." To spite me, they would then do the very thing I suggested they refrain from doing. But when their parents were delighted to see their children making progress in school, they would turn and spite the parents all over again.

Erik Erikson, the noted child psychologist and psychoanalyst, coined the term *negative identity* to describe the many adolescents who are sensitive to what their parents demand and do exactly the opposite, wishing to be loved for themselves, not for their accomplishments. Children of a number of college professors become dropouts; sons of professional athletes shun sports and take to literature and music. I know at least a dozen children of Orthodox rabbis who married Gentiles.

Failure, when studied carefully, frequently reveals an attempt to hurt those who have nurtured us in a way that stirred up our hatred and resentment. Parents were either too distant and cold, holding back love and caring, or were so overbearing that the child was unable to develop his own personality.

For a number of children and adults failure means "getting even" with parents who in some way have prevented them from existing in an atmosphere of understanding and peacefulness. Children may swiftly bury their early rage, knowing they have to rely on parents for survival. But if they do not face up to and understand that rage in later years, it is apt to smoulder the rest of their unhappy lives.

The Child Within Us All

One reason for failure rarely acknowledged is the strong need all of us possess to identify with our parents. If a mother or a father is a ne'er-do-well, a child feels he must become one too. A man who consulted me, Richard, possessed many strengths but could not permit himself to succeed in investment banking because he felt he should not make a better living than his father had. Every time this man thought of a creative project, he rejected it. To outstrip his father meant abandoning him.

All of us, no matter what our age, still remain in part the child who ardently wishes for his parents' love and approval, even if they have died. Their early attitudes and the way they raised us remain in the deepest parts of our mind. We still hear them talking to us, commanding us, as they did when we were small children.

Another kind of failure, rarely discussed, is one in which we try to please those who have clearly shown they *want* us to fail. Many a mother who has not been a success does not wish her daughter to succeed and show her up. Many a father feels the same way about a son. The wish that the child fail may apply not only to the child of the same sex, for mothers may become threatened by their sons' achievements and fathers by their daughters' attainments. Such parents cannot tolerate seeing their children succeed because the parents, in the part of them that still remains a child, feel jealous of and competitive with their offspring. I often note this attitude in my clinical work.

One patient, May, a physician, became very depressed each time she felt successful in her work. She had grown up with a mother who could not bear her daughter's beauty or femininity, for she had wanted a son. When my patient was only four, her mother cut her hair to make her look more boyish. When she did well in school, her mother belittled her high marks. When she started to date, her mother, out of strong competition, tried to stop young men from pursuing her daughter.

I helped May realize she was unconsciously trying to gratify her mother by failing all the time, thus keeping the relationship intact. Rather than risk having her mother hate her or demean her, my patient would fail and feel miserable. She had never accepted a man's proposal, though she had had several.

Each time Gerald thought of leaving a menial job and moving to a better one, he recalled the admonitions of his arrogant father, who warned him as a boy, "Gerald, you'll never amount to anything, you don't have the stamina." Like most children, Gerald wanted to carry out his father's prediction and keep him happy. A child's life depends on the parent, both psychologically and physically, and even part of us as adults still reasons that we need our parents' approval even if the parents are deceased.

In Gerald's case, though his father had been dead for fifteen years, the little boy within him kept his father's voice alive and clear. Parental orders from childhood remain imprinted on our minds as long as we live. We feel, erroneously, that if we do not obey these voices we should be punished. We may arrange that punishment either by failing or feeling miserable, or both.

Failure has many faces. In the course of my work with college students I noted unique types of failure that emerged in people overwhelmed by parents. If parents and other relatives whom we have been close to give us an exaggerated view of ourselves, one that is unrealistic, we are likely to assume that the whole world is our oyster and that we should be treated like a king or queen, or at least a prince or princess.

A twenty-year-old man, thrown out of college in his sophomore year, sought me out for help because of his deep depression. As a boy Robert had been consistently told by his parents that he was a genius, an athletic star, and deserving of love and admiration from everyone. When he entered college he found there were other young men and women as bright, if not brighter, and as personable, if not more so. For many years Robert's contention that the world owed him a living had not gotten him into trouble, but at college it did. He found he would have to work for what he wanted. In his counseling experience with me, I had to help him tone down his arrogance and his grandiose notions, and help him accept that he was more human than otherwise.

Sometimes we fail because we are not willing to work for success, as Robert learned. Many unhappy husbands and wives fail in marriage because they are convinced they should be loved regardless of how provocative or belligerent they are. Many an employee is fired because he believes he deserves praise without working for it.

There is a little of Robert in all of us, something that

keeps wanting love and praise without the expenditure of any effort by us. This philosophy leads to failure, for we have to work for almost everything in life—a successful marriage, a job we yearn for, the love of a child, a safe universe.

Perhaps we fail most often because the child in us is always alive and because we evaluate the world, in large part, through that child's eyes and ears. Even if our parents are dead, we hear their voices and visualize them constantly in our dreams and fantasies, sometimes disguised, sometimes recognizable.

If we dare think of changing the way we live to a style vastly different from the way we were brought up, we may invoke the words of parents who pleaded, "Don't leave me, stay near me, I need you." We don't realize that a life of success and pleasure entails to some degree the abandonment of the parents.

One of my patients felt she had killed her mother because when her mother asked her, an only child, if she would live with her in a small house, she replied, "I can't live with anyone, I have to exist in a place all my own." A few months later her mother was taken to an old persons' home and died within a year. It took the patient almost two years to feel she had not murdered her mother, that her mother's dependency was not of her daughter's making.

Few adults accept the fact that there lives within them a little child who still views life as though he were four or five years old, his parents by his side, ordering him to do or not do certain acts, to think in certain ways, and to always be obedient. To understand our failures and overcome them, we need to know what the child in ourselves is thinking. All failures, in one way or another, are caused by our reluctance to face the child within.

If a youngster has been told consistently, "Perform and

I will love you," as an adult he will feel angry and spiteful because he wishes to be loved just for being himself. We do not want to please parental images and voices that demand good performances from us but often feel we have no choice. We do not want to feel hated or risk feeling abandoned by a parent.

As adults, if we wish to be happy and successful in whatever our undertaking, we need to ask, "Why do we work so hard to keep parental voices alive? Why do we comply with all our hearts to a parent's demands, then resent it?" The answer is that the child within remains a vulnerable part of us, for the child feels small and weak. Many who fail do not realize that they allow the vulnerable child inside to gain ascendancy over the adult way of thinking and behaving. We can use the mature, adult part of us to listen and talk to the fragile child, to help him understand why he wants to fight with his mother or father, why he turns colleagues and friends into siblings or supervisors into tyrannical parents. We can help the child within eventually understand how he distorts the present and allows the past to control him.

We need to help the child in us know that he often turns the adult sexual partner into a parent, then feels guilty about enjoying spontaneous sex and cripples himself emotionally. What the child in us needs to hear from the mature part of ourselves is that sexual fantasies toward parents are normal, natural, and universal. We do not have to punish ourselves for experiencing them for they are part of the human condition.

It is a fact of psychological life that when we listen to and talk empathetically with the child in us we become capable of more mature behavior and do not have to punish ourselves when we become successful. Our inner child needs attention and conversation to help us become happier and more achieving adults. For it is this child who makes us feel distrustful and angry, directs us unwittingly to arrange for our failures, urges us to refuse to cooperate in love and work, and interferes with our ability to succeed.

The child within sees the world as full of Goliaths threatening helpless little Davids. If we permit the little David in us to gain ascendency we feel surrounded by vicious, tyrannical forces. But if we recognize that the child in us is only a part of us, which we can control once we understand this aspect of ourselves, then we can act successfully in the world of adults. We have to realize, too, that the people we fear the most, originally our parents, also have a little child within, directing much of their lives.

Sometimes it is difficult to recognize and accept that a formidable boss, a tyrannical teacher, or an authoritarian father is governed by his childhood wishes. But it's true. President Bush has such a little boy within, and Queen Elizabeth a little girl. Those who intimidate us the most turn out to be quite similar to us when we accept this truth.

Our inner child is the major actor in our dreams and fantasies as well as the engine that makes our emotional machine either work well or sink into apathy and depression. It is this phenomenon that we will discuss and develop throughout the challenging journey ahead.

CHAPTER 2

RESOLVING FAILURES IN LOVE, SEX, AND MARRIAGE

No relationship yields more failures than the love, sex, and marital relationships between men and women. Starting with Adam and Eve and continuing into the 1990s, there *never* has been a golden age of love and marriage.

Couples who start off blissfully happy, ostensibly loving each other, frequently end up hating, abusing, and sometimes killing each other. In his book *Road to Divorce,* Lawrence Stone calls ours a divorcing society. While the popularity of marriage may still be growing, the propensity to break up is developing even faster. Divorce has increased drastically in the past century; it is now estimated that over 50 percent of all marriages in this country end in divorce.

Not only do marriages collapse but many men and women who continue to live together frequently feel they have made a mistake. Hatred and misery can be endured for years as an unhappy couple dwell under the same roof. In the play and movie *Who's Afraid of Virginia Woolf?* a married couple remained together for twenty years, castigating and demeaning each other all the while.

Why are there so many failures in love, sex, and marriage? In what ways can these failures be reduced so that love, sex, and marriage can be enjoyable rather than a distasteful burden?

A major reason love relationships deteriorate is that the wife and husband do not understand what "falling in love" is all about. Very few are aware that it is a childish, highly subjective, irrational act. Though billions have experienced it, it is never based on reasonable, thoughtful behavior.

Sociologists who study why specific mates are chosen conclude, not surprisingly, that those who fall in love and marry are usually of similar age and socioeconomic status, and they are often of the same race and religion. Sociologists also point out that the likelihood of two persons falling in love increases if they live near each other, work in the same place, and possess similar political and social values.

Philosophers have written of love, and their thoughts about it are quite instructive. Early Romans concluded, "Amare et sapere deis non conceditur"—the ability to keep one's wits when in love is not granted to the gods. In our era George Santayana has referred to falling in love as that "deep and dumb instinctive affinity." The psychologist Carl Jung, describing the bliss of falling in love, wrote, "You see that girl, you get a seizure, you are caught." The anthropologist Ralph Linton described the ecstasy and madness in a love affair as similar to an epileptic fit.

These statements about falling in love suggest how truly subjective the process is, how very irrational we are when we're head over heels in love, and how very nonrational we can be when it comes to love and marriage.

When we fall in love we seriously distort the loved one, making him or her the epitome of all we yearn for, all we hoped we would ever be, the perfect nurturing parent who will always take care of us. Falling in love carries with it an overestimation of the loved one—he is the perfect man or she is the perfect woman.

Almost everyone falling in love or observing those in love overlooks how infantile the process is. Indeed, its roots lie in infancy. Psychologists have demonstrated that the prototype of falling in love is a child, or more accurately an infant, sucking at the mother's breast.

The bliss lovers feel, the intensity, the passion they express emerges because they are convinced they have finally found the ideal parent who will open up a paradise they believed lost and cure them of all ills, all aches and pains.

The person in love turns his partner into a dreamlike figure who gratifies primitive wishes that can never be fulfilled in reality.

A thirty-year-old woman, a newspaper reporter, came to me after her year-old marriage to another reporter had failed. She complained, "He treated me as though I were a baby and he was the mother who knew best. I felt my life was not my own. I couldn't breathe without his telling me how." She eventually realized she had sought a parental figure who would take care of her and order her around, as her mother and father had. The child within searched constantly for the caretakers of early days, unaware of their faults, especially their domineering qualities.

It is important to recognize the highly subjective, childish nature of falling in love because so many lovers and most husbands and wives falsely believe that the bliss and passion of the dream of love can continue indefinitely.

Love's supposed ability to sustain all that is charged to the power of love is one of the most unrealistic wishes with which every adult must eventually come to terms. Marriage and other love relationships fail mainly because we expect our partners to gratify until death our primitive desires. Although at some point we give lip service to the idea that the honeymoon is over, most—perhaps all of us—erroneously believe romantic love can endure to the grave.

How Love Turns to Hate

We overlook the fact, one that no two lovers seem to face, that no two people can depend on each other for everything. If lovers and young married couples could be helped to accept that in every relationship there will be inevitable disillusionment, the self-abnegation that exists in the disappointed lover would be less pervasive and so would the subsequent hatred.

When any two persons live with each other, particularly two lovers or man and wife, the demands of daily existence always intrude. Each partner slowly gives less and focuses more on his own needs. The coincidence of giving less and expecting more punctures romantic love. It sparks hatred, mutual recrimination, and the virtual end of the relationship.

To avoid failures in love, sex, and marriage, we have to accept that the state of bliss is a short-term affair, with only intermittent awakenings, and that ecstasy does not often occur except when we feel omnipotent as babies in the arms of our mother.

Love relationships also fail because both partners try to be all-powerful kings and queens. Each one resents the other for demanding he give rather than receive. Neither understands that the demands he makes on the other are high—some impossible to fulfill.

John and Sally, a couple in their early thirties, came to see me for marital counseling after a year's marriage. An attractive husband and wife, with responsible jobs in a large public relations firm, they described a deeply loving courtship, then a blissful honeymoon.

Sally said in the first consultation, "As soon as I saw John, I knew he was the man for me."

Famous last words, I thought to myself, words I have heard so often.

Sally described John as tall, dark, and handsome, polished, bright, articulate, sexy, warm, and tender. I thought, How can you beat that in a husband?

John smiled as he listened to this description, then he said, "When I first saw Sally's beautiful smile and warm demeanor, I knew this was the girl for me. As I talked to her, her words were like pearls of wisdom. Her very touch really sent me."

In subsequent sessions I learned that both came from homes where their parents fought constantly and that each felt divided loyalties as they related to their parents. While John and Sally shared a closeness and kinship because of the similarity of their backgrounds, they did not realize they were overestimating each other, believing they had secured the perfect parent who would protect them from their respective vulnerabilities.

Both courtship and honeymoon offered the reassurance they craved. They enjoyed the closeness a mother and infant show during the first few months of a baby's life, in which both partners feel as one person. Like many lovers who imagine they are one, John and Sally constantly referred to each other as "the better half."

But, as with all adult relationships, the demands of reality intruded: neither could sustain the illusion of being the perfect nurturer. Slowly, as each felt more deprived and misunderstood, resentment supplanted love. Power struggles instead of mutual cooperation became the order of the day.

In my work with John and Sally I helped them realize that each felt like a vulnerable child whose needs were not understood by the other. I reassured them that neither was required to give as much as either imagined, but I also pointed out that neither could ever receive as much love and reassurance as they longed for. They had to face up to their unrealistic expectations.

John and Sally learned how to succeed in marriage when they could finally understand the child in themselves and thus tolerate the child in their partner. If other marital partners could do this there would be far fewer failures in love and marriage.

We Write Our Own Scripts

Another reason so many marriages fail is that only happy people can embark on happy relationships. Most of us erroneously believe that a lover is a cure-all, that he will somehow nurture and support us so that nothing could possibly hurt or anger us.

If a person shows many vulnerabilities and conflicts, no lover can cure them. Marilyn Monroe was considered one of the most beautiful and gifted women in the world, but all the reassurances and adulation she received from men like Joe DiMaggio and Arthur Miller could not cure her of her damaged self-image.

Neither Marilyn nor the average person who needs reassurance should expect a love partner to resolve inner turmoil. We have to face our own self-doubts and self-recriminations. Marilyn tried to do this when she finally went to two prominent psychoanalysts. She sought them too late in her tragic life because she was unable to give up the drinking and the sleeping pills that by then seemed necessary for her very existence. Many believe that she deliberately took an overdose after a brief affair with Robert Kennedy, then attorney general.

In my work with unhappy married couples, which now spans four decades, I have learned that a chronic marital complaint is really an unconscious wish. The man who complains, "My wife is a cold, frigid bitch," really wants such a woman. A warm, responsive, sexual woman would frighten him. Similarly, a wife who constantly berates her husband as weak and passive unconsciously wants a weak man. A strong, assertive man would frighten her.

When I treated Robert, a man in his late thirties, who lived with Jane, twenty-eight, he constantly criticized her as hypercritical and asexual. But as I reviewed his behavior with Jane, it became clear how often he provoked her to criticize him, which automatically made him uninterested in her as a sexual partner.

As Robert realized how often he behaved like a belligerent son in Jane's presence and ceased some of his provocative behavior, she become more receptive and sexual. Yet Robert still could not tolerate her sexually and, feeling like a submissive little boy in the presence of an overpowering mother, became impotent.

One of the salient reasons many love relationships fail is that most people, like Robert, are afraid to love. They view loving as submitting, cooperation as yielding, and devotion as ignoble masochism.

In my work with countless numbers of both divorced and single men and women who cannot sustain a love relationship, I have observed that many distort love relationships, contending that when immersed in them they feel like acquiescent children. This emerges in their relationship with me as they come to think that to cooperate with me and take responsibility for their own lives makes them feel like a weak enemy surrendering to the opposition.

It is not widely understood that two people sufficiently attracted to each other to start a committed relationship are really quite similar. They complement each other's immaturities and idiosyncracies. There is a sadist for every masochist, a detached, obsessive partner for every clinging vine, a persistent rejector for every lover who wants constant reassurance.

Although lovers and marital couples are the last to recognize it, they mirror parts of each other. I have never met a wife who hated sex who did not have a husband who had several sexual inhibitions. I have always found that the husband who was alcoholic was married to a woman who aided and abetted the alcoholism and vicariously participated in it by taking pleasure in watching him imbibe, though she would be the last to admit it.

When a person marries, a strong part of that person wants to be a cherished child. Who can cherish us more than a perfect mother or father? The problem is that as we unconsciously make our partner into the mother or father or both, we begin to relate to them as if they *were* the parents of our past. This means they also become the recipients of our hatreds, resentments, jealousies, and deprivations.

Perhaps one of the most negative consequences of turning a spouse into a parental figure is that we then feel like small children facing gargantuan adults. Along with these earlier feelings arise the old self-doubts, the shaky self-image, the lack of confidence, and the inevitable sexual problems. For if we make our spouse into a parental figure, sex feels uncomfortable if not unacceptable.

Many a marital partner, while venting his spleen on his mate, is unaware that he is making the mate a figure, or figures, of the past and is using his hatred to protect himself against feeling like a vulnerable child.

Several years ago Harold, a man in his forties, with two daughters and an attractive wife, came for therapy. He announced that he was sexually impotent with his wife but potent with his mistress. He referred to his wife, Rebecca, as looking precisely like his mother and acting like her.

Harold lamented, "Every morning when we wake up she smells like my mother, and I feel a noose tighten around my neck."

In contrast to his wife, he said his mistress made him appear strong and virile, adding, "There's no noose there." But as he continued his relationship with her, she suddenly demanded more time and attention. She pressured him to spend a week in Atlantic City. During this vacation she cooked, sewed, and assumed many of the traditional wifely responsibilities. He now found he was impotent with her, too, as she, in his fantasy, turned into his mother, with whom sex was forbidden.

Although pained by this experience, Harold became aware that every time he had lived with a woman he turned her into a "big mommy" and himself into a little boy, then became impotent. It took several years of treatment for him to realize that he wrote his own script. He was reluctant to be a man with a woman, preferring the earlier reality of being a little boy with a big, forbidden mama.

Why Forbidden Sex Attracts

Extramarital affairs are so prevalent because so many married men and women can enjoy sex only when it appears forbidden. In my practice of psychotherapy I have often heard statements like "A motel is so much more of a turn-on than the bedroom my wife and I share," "When I'm far away from my husband I feel like an adventurer excited about new scenes and vistas." "I enjoy sex with my mistress in the back of a taxi more than with my wife on a comfortable bed."

Because marriage sanctions sex, for many people it takes the so-called fun out of doing what is forbidden. Frequently husbands and wives complain that the sexual act is experienced as a chore performed for a mother or father.

Children do have strong sexual yearnings toward parents, which they renounce to become good little girls and good little boys. But, as we have emphasized, in later years many married couples experience their partners as mothers and fathers for whom they must again be good little girls and good little boys. Just as children defy parents and disobey parental sanctions, many married persons enjoy defying marital sanctions and derive pleasure from rebelling against their spouses. They enjoy rebellion for the sake of rebellion.

James, a married man who told me he hated being in or out of bed with his "sad" wife, sought therapy because whenever he attempted sex he became impotent. He indulged in a number of extramarital affairs that always occurred out of town. Both James and I learned something very important as he discussed his affairs.

The farther he went from home with another woman, the more potent he became. Distance, in his mind, meant farther away from the ruling mother-wife. The more rebellious he felt, the more relaxed he became in bed. Like anyone who turns his marital partner into a parental figure and then finds sex forbidden, James saw lovemaking with his wife as a command performance—as if he were an obedient child performing for an exacting mother.

Over 50 percent of married people today are involved in extramarital affairs. We have to view these men and women as failing in marriage and beset with emotional problems. Unable to commit themselves to a full-time relationship, they feel constricted by it, squelched and controlled.

The man in an extramarital affair is usually unable to take on the necessary tolerance of frustration required of a mature, married person. Instead, he indulges himself consistently with other sexual partners. He cannot empathize with his marital partner; he feels that empathy is ignoble surrender and cooperation is a helpless defeat. The same is true of the woman in an extramarital affair.

To succeed in a marital relationship both partners have to genuinely accept the limitations every person in the world possesses. Most of us, perhaps all of those involved in extramarital affairs, instead pine for an omnipotent parent who will take complete care of us, nurturing us as if we still were very young children.

Often the married person involves himself or herself in a new relationship because marriage has come to seem too much of an unhappy commitment. Switching between marital partner and lover yields a feeling of pseudoindependence, as if to say "I don't really need anyone that much. I can play the field. I will be indebted to no one sexually."

What neither of these wives or husbands can admit is that they need two people to diffuse the intensity of a committed relationship; one relationship feels like a noose around the neck. They are actually frightened children running from a commitment, feeling small, weak, overpowered in marriage.

The married person involved in affair after affair fails to master the psychological tasks every mature person must face. We should be able to depend on another human being without feeling like a helpless child. We should also permit another human being to depend on us without feeling like a compliant slave.

The mature person can cooperate with a mate without power struggles. He can accept childlike sexual fantasies in himself and in his partner without becoming overwhelmed or feeling he deserves punishment. Most failures in marriage occur because partners possess the tendency to turn their mates into parental figures. This distortion of the mate, unconscious though it is, provokes many difficulties between wife and husband.

First, the old resentments and vengeful feelings that belong to the past are discharged in the present. The married person who has felt unloved and cruelly treated, perhaps neglected, by parents, has a strong tendency to view the marital partner in the same way and then vent his rage. He often hurls out the words in anger: "You remind me of my mother," or "You're just like my impossible father." He does not realize the complainant writes his own script as he turns an essentially innocent victim into a villain.

Making the spouse into the parent of the past destroys marital happiness, particularly in the sexual relationship.

If a man turns his wife into a mother, he feels extreme guilt because he believes he indulges in incest. This is probably the main reason for impotence in men: they unconsciously see the wife as a mother figure and are overwhelmed by guilt.

Similarly, when the woman makes her husband the father, she is apt to renounce the pleasures of sex because having sex with her father is taboo. I worked with a married woman in therapy, Mary, who told me that the only way she could enjoy herself sexually was to imagine that her husband was her former boyfriend or a man in her current work life or a movie star. By renouncing her sexual interest in her husband, whom in fantasy she made her father, and replacing him in fantasy with someone else, she could enjoy sex with him. Mary felt too guilty to embark on an extramarital affair but by imagining herself with someone other than her husband, she could undertake the fantasied extramarital affair.

Parents exert a powerful effect on us even though most of us deny their impact. Men and women who do not marry often feel that their first loyalty is to one or both parents. Instead of nurturing and loving a spouse, these persons feel guilty when they indulge in an affair or embark on a marital life far away from their parents, as though they were deserting them. The chain between parent and child can be an enduring one if too many impossible demands have been made on the child early in life.

Many a single adult can in fantasy turn a mother or father into a marital partner and live with the parent the rest of their lives. I recall a middle-aged man in therapy, Douglas, intelligent and attractive, who lived with his aged father and rarely dated women. To leave his father and enjoy a life apart from him was to Douglas "like leaving a beloved wife and saying 'I'm divorcing you to be with somebody else.' That's much too cruel."

As Douglas eventually realized, the father aided and abetted this strong attachment. He became aware that he was making his beloved father into a mate in order to satisfy his father. Still dependent on papa, he had lacked the psychic strength to embark on a life of his own.

Failures in love relationships, particularly sexual relationships, occur because those who cannot enjoy themselves sexually do not understand their childhood fantasies. They do not accept the fact that to enjoy the self sexually one has to be able to regress and enjoy the child within and the child in one's partner. All too many of us, for instance, fail to recognize that the kissing and hugging in the initial stages of lovemaking are reminiscent of a baby in a mother's arms. This is why lovers frequently refer to each other as baby or babe and often use baby talk.

Not only do sexual partners have to enjoy the child within and in their partner for sex to be enjoyable but they have to recognize that cooperation does not mean submission. Many lovers equate the sexual act with performing a chore for a parent, much like producing a bowel movement. I have worked with countless men and women who refer to making love as putting out, much as one puts out for a parent, whether it be bowel movement or other chores.

To enjoy making love we have to understand that our partner is like the parent of the opposite sex but is also a person in his own right. This may be difficult because we are all inclined at crucial moments to turn ourselves into children and our partners into exacting parents. When two people can each accept the child in themselves and in the other as well as the adult in the self and in the partner, then tender and erotic feelings join in an enjoyable, loving relationship.

A happy marriage is made by two happy human beings. Most of those who argue against the institution of marriage fail to recognize that many people who marry are psychologically immature children. Because any intimacy frightens them, they must protect themselves from feeling too close to anyone for too long a time. The fate of an unhappy marriage has been decided long before the marriage occurs. The human psyche is formed in early childhood, and it remains enshrined in the person without his conscious knowledge.

Most of those who rebel against marriage are deeply unhappy men and women. It often takes a long time for unhappily married spouses to take responsibility for their own misery. Like revengeful children they ascribe the difficulties either to the institution of marriage or to a sadistic, unfeeling spouse. There would be many more happy marriages if unhappy spouses could acknowledge their contributions to an impossible marital arrangement, the offshoot of their fantasies and fears as they grew up.

CHAPTER 3

EMOTIONAL WOUNDS OF CHILDHOOD

Millions of parents and children suffer constant turmoil in their relationships with each other without understanding the causes. Mutual hatred, often very intense, appears to be pervasive among parents and children throughout our culture.

The rate of child abuse keeps soaring and childhood and teenage depression increases. Suicide rates among teenagers mount. Parents are driven to kill their children, and some children murder their parents. A particularly brutal case occurred in February of 1991, when a youth who had been adopted as a baby murdered his mother and father. A few months after he was adopted, his mother became pregnant, bore a boy, who evidently in the murderer's mind received far more love than he did. Eventually he got even with what he believed to be his unloving parents.

Murders within the home have reached a new high. Unhappy children, some as young as nine or ten, get caught up in the drug culture and often, in the grip of drugs, will harm parents and siblings.

If the family is supposed to be an institution society created to bring pleasure to its members through mutual love, emotional security, and self-confidence, then both the American society and the American family have failed. As parents and children become alienated, the family of the 1990s is frequently referred to as fragmented.

Parent and Child

Until about one hundred years ago the child was viewed chiefly as a slave of his parents. The history of childhood is one of abuse, torment, and sadism. But by the turn of the twentieth century our views toward the growing child were dramatically modified. Progressive education, the mental health movement, and dynamic psychology influenced parents, teachers, and others to take an active part in the care of children. It was now recognized that children were highly vulnerable in many ways and should be protected, sometimes against the cruelty of their own parents.

By the early 1940s TLC (tender loving care) was seen as essential for all children. We also learned that children go through unique phases of development and that the most desirable atmosphere for them is a family in which two parents who love and respect each other work together to enhance the child's emotional and social growth.

From the so-called age of the child, which lasted until the early 1960s, we moved to what has been dubbed the age of narcissism. Self-help books now urge us to be our own best friend. *I* takes precedence over *we* or *they*. The welfare of children is on the decline. We see the latchkey child come home five days a week to an empty abode.

Infants are taken to pre-nursery schools at one-and-a-half years old, when they are barely out of the cradle. The role of mother has been demeaned. Today a woman is accorded much more status and prestige if she takes care of adults in a corporation than if she nurtures children at home.

How and why do so many parent-child relationships of the 1990s fail? What can be done to improve them and help youngsters and teenagers mature in a more enjoyable, productive manner?

To answer these questions we must first answer a prior one: "Why do men and women want to have children?" Several answers seem relevant. For one, to have a child is socially sanctioned: the Bible tells us to be fruitful and multiply. Although this belief has been modified somewhat during the last few decades, many husbands and wives, as well as single men and women, still consider themselves failures if they do not become parents. Thus parenting fulfills social expectations.

Being a parent usually enhances sexual identity. Men delight in distributing cigars to male friends right after a baby is born. Women feel proud of giving birth and are usually pleased to talk about their pregnancy. Most prospective parents consciously or unconsciously look forward to living their lives all over again by providing the child with opportunities and advantages they themselves lacked as children—love, wealth, education, self-esteem, or anything the parent wished for in earlier years but did not receive.

When men and women decide to become parents they are in one way or another trying to enhance themselves. If more parents could accept the fact that parenthood can be experienced as a pleasure as well as a responsibility, perhaps more mothers and fathers would feel less resentful of their children.

Very often in my therapeutic work with mothers and fathers I hear parenthood considered exclusively as a demanding chore. When anything is viewed as a chore the person naturally will wish to avoid it. Perhaps our age of the child gave many parents the distorted view that children should receive pleasure but were not expected to provide their parents with any. Maybe one of the reasons we moved from the age of the child to the age of narcissism is that parents were resentful at not being sufficiently appreciated as parents and were not enjoying their parental tasks.

While many factors influence the growth and development of a child, the most crucial is the parent-child relationship. The ongoing relationship of a child with his parents is the most important variable in determining how the youngster will later emerge as an adult human being, whether he will be primarily self-confident and loving or depressed and angry.

Again I must stress that it is a matter of degree. All of us will feel at times the touch of depression and anger, for a life devoid of such emotions simply doesn't exist. But when the touch changes into a constant overflow of depression and hatred, this is a clue that the person is suffering deeply because of early unhappy relationships with that person's parents.

Parent-child successes and failures start much earlier than most of us realize. They originate at the moment of conception. If a child is conceived in an atmosphere of warmth and love, the feelings the parents show toward each other will affect the growth and development of the fetus. How the prospective mother feels mentally and physically during her nine months of pregnancy will determine in many ways how the infant will emerge at birth. Research documents the fact that premature births, brain damage, and other physical handicaps are in many ways influenced by how supportive and loving the prospective mother felt during the pregnancy.

If the prospective mother undergoes stress of any kind during the first three months of pregnancy, the infant may be born with a cleft palate. Failures at birth, including the most dramatic, the death of the baby, are often related to how well nourished the prospective mother is emotionally and physically. Economically and emotionally deprived women, particularly those without mates, are more inclined to produce handicapped infants than women who are economically and emotionally secure. If a prospective mother is addicted to alcohol or drugs, her infant, in all probability, will not emerge in the best emotional, physical, or intellectual condition.

The birth process itself has an impact on the success or failure of the parent-child relationship. If the mother has the benefit of a warm, attending physician, a benign nurse, and, perhaps most important, a loving husband, the birth process will probably be easier and the infant will have a better chance of emerging with all faculties intact.

Parents, being human, always have preferences and biases. If husband and wife desperately wanted a son but a daughter emerges, her chances of a happy life are at once lessened. If the prospective parents want a girl and a boy is born, he too is destined to have many uncomfortable moments.

It is emotionally healthy for parents to have their preferences and to voice them to each other, to family, and to friends. It is no crime to want a blond, blue-eyed daughter or a sturdy, muscular boy. The more that prospective parents have an opportunity to discuss their respective biases with each other and empathize as they face their own prejudices, the happier the child will tend to become. If the parents' preferences are shrouded in secrecy, if the parents subtly and indirectly act out their resentments and create a tense atmosphere, their child will suffer.

A young woman in her late twenties, Elizabeth, came to me for help when her son was six months old. She appeared depressed and irritable; she complained that she had lost much sleep and lacked an appetite. I discovered that she had been raised in a family where her older brother was the favored child. Though she was not aware of her buried resentment toward him or her parents, it did not take much encouragement on my part for her to voice her conviction that she had never felt appreciated as a growing girl.

Elizabeth was eventually able to tell me, with guilt and shame in her voice, "I really must confess that I wanted a baby girl, someone I could love the way I wanted to be loved in spite of being a girl. Instead, I gave birth to a boy. It was as if I had given birth to my brother, the preferred one, who, I admit, I hated at times."

After Elizabeth gradually discharged her resentments toward her brother and parents and when she could accept permission from me to have preferred a daughter, she eventually relaxed and gave far more love and attention to her son.

Parents can help children more easily develop into successful human beings if they are truthful in talking to their marital partner about their preferences. If parents understand each other's feelings, the child is off to a far more successful start than if his parents are endlessly but silently at odds.

Anyone who has worked with parents in counseling recognizes that all parents in their relationship with their children recapitulate their own childhood. At each stage of the child's development mothers and fathers relive what transpired when they were at that stage. If they understand this, it almost guarantees that their child's emotional life will be much easier.

Although most parents wish to provide their sons and daughters with a better life than they experienced, this is more readily wished for than achieved. It is not easy for a father who was drilled and pressured to become a superathlete to allow his son to play ball just for the fun of it. It is not easy for a mother to withhold criticism of her young daughter for not dressing fashionably if her parents had expected her to be a fashion plate.

To be loving and mature parents, mothers and fathers have to be able to understand their own childhood resentments. They have to accept the fact that their parents had limitations and made mistakes. George Santayana tells us that those who have not learned the lessons of history are bound to repeat its failures. Mothers and fathers who still idealize their parents or are intimidated unduly by their early images of them and their voices will make the same mistakes with their children that their parents made with them. This is an emotional heritage all of us have to confront to some degree.

I worked in psychotherapy with a physician pressured by his parents as a boy to become "my son, the doctor." He sought help because his son, despite a high intelligence, had become a failure academically. It took several months for me to help Dr. Miller recognize that his son Jeff was rebelling against the same kind of parental pressure that Dr. Miller's parents had exerted on him.

I still find it fascinating to observe that when parents gain some understanding of their own conflicts with their parents and then are able to move an emotional distance from them, their children prosper emotionally. When Dr. Miller could share with me the hurt and resentment he felt toward his exacting parents and later could forgive them for their neuroses, he became a happier man and easily conveyed this new happiness to his son. The latter in turn no longer felt pressured to perform and was far happier too.

What I observed with Dr. Miller and his son I have observed hundreds of times with other parents. When they could face the unhappy child within themselves, they could relate much better to their sons or daughters.

It is crucial for parents to get in touch with the child in themselves because, more than anything else, it is that child who influences their behavior as parents. When I was a child therapist I helped Norman, a boy who could hardly speak. He was what mental health professionals call autistic.

I learned that when Norman was born his mother felt very depressed, hardly talked to him, rarely held him close. As I worked with her, I discovered she had spent most of her childhood in an orphanage where she received little or no love or attention. I helped her face the slings and arrows of her "outrageous" past. Slowly she became able to give Norman the care and understanding I showed her, care and understanding that had been missing in her early life. I concluded that while Norman's own therapy was helpful, my work with his mother, who then modified her way of relating to him, was more crucial than anything else that occurred in their therapy.

Although the causes of childhood autism are controversial and still being debated, many autistic children can be helped if they and their parents are given the necessary emotional nourishment.

When a child is born a father may become very jealous of the close relationship between his wife and the infant.

Even though fathers are now becoming more of an equal partner in childrearing, the infant is still mainly in the hands of the mother, and many fathers need permission to face their normal jealousy when mothers are taken over by another lover, so to speak. If a father as a child had a younger brother or sister who took his mother's or his father's attention away from him, then jealousy of his child may be quite intense. His rage may be disruptive to both the child's well-being and his wife's.

Failures in early childhood could be dramatically lessened if parents permitted themselves to face a change that occurs after the birth of a baby. All parents start a new relationship when a child arrives, and with each addition to the family the parents' relationship changes. A second child may remind the mother or father of a younger or older brother or sister, and an early, unresolved rivalry toward a sibling may show itself in the attitude toward their own child.

Parents in our society are not concerned enough about the difficulties that ensue when one or more children come along. There would be fewer failures in parent-child relationships if parents could be honest with themselves and each other about the resentment, jealousy, hurt and, at times, despair that all children at one point or another inevitably induce in their mothers and fathers.

The Power of Parents

In their day-to-day behavior with their children, directly or indirectly parents define for the child the meaning of success and failure. Whether we acknowledge it or not, parents make clear what is acceptable or unacceptable, ideal or forbidden. Many parents believe that only when their child is an achiever is he successful. They applaud his *A*s and highly disapprove of any grade less than a *B*. The father who emphasizes achievement, who expects his son to hit home runs consistently, and if he strikes out gives the son a contemptuous, demeaning stare, is withholding love from his son.

As we study parent-child relationships, we discover that the seeds of failure or success are planted early in the child's life. Who the child becomes is in many ways determined by how his parents have defined success and failure and how well he has been able to adapt to their values.

Some parents define success as receiving accolades or in one way or another becoming popular. If a child proves to be unpopular, such a parent may feel denigrated and may communicate his disapproval to the child. Other parents define success as performing good deeds and the child, to earn his parent's love and to feel worthy, will devote himself to benefiting others.

When a child loses a parent's love he tends to lose respect for himself. An extreme example of bad parent-child relationships can be seen in the case of Willie, in prison for life for murdering two men on the subways of New York City and for almost killing a guard in prison. He never knew his father, who left home before the boy was born and shortly after went to prison for several murders. Willie grew up as a boy feeling that his father would not have deserted him had he loved him. He also heard his mother and grandmother, with whom he lived, often rebuke him with the words, "You're going to be just like your father." Subconsciously Willie decided to carry out what seemed to him a command.

Every child absorbs his parents *do*s and *don't*s and judges himself according to how well he lives up to his parents' standards. Most parents want their children to be winners, be it at school, on the ball field, or among friends. The overwhelming pressure of these demands, spoken or unspoken, may drive many children to seek to be losers. They find out what their parents wish from them and then do the opposite in rebellion. Such parents do not realize that when they insist that some kind of success is necessary for the child to gain his parents' love, they unwittingly promote misery, depression, and lack of self-esteem in the child.

Many famous people who have been achievers are unhappy, hate themselves, and on occasion kill themselves, feeling totally unloved. All of Vincent van Gogh's attempts to support himself and stay alive failed. He finally became psychotic, slashed off one ear, and soon committed suicide. After he died, this highly gifted man was acknowledged as the father of Expressionism and was considered one of the leading artists of all time. We can point to many men and women who are internationally recognized, applauded by millions, who hated themselves, in some cases killed themselves. Among them are Ernest Hemingway and Marilyn Monroe, mentioned earlier.

Countless children are punished and hated by parents because they do not eat a certain food at a certain time, as though the parent's life depended on this act. Other children are castigated and demeaned because they have not moved their bowels regularly or performed some chore the parent feels must be carried out at once.

Many parents fail to realize that children enjoy achieving and do not fight rules and regulations at home or at school when they feel that regardless of their performances they are considered worthy of staying alive and being loved. The suicides of many children are due to the feeling that their parents don't care what becomes of them.

If a child hates himself, he has first felt his parent's disapproval communicated by verbal or physical beatings or by a hostile and rejecting stare. Smiling, successful children are those whose parents succeeded in constantly smiling at them.

Too many parents voice the sentiment of former football coach of the Green Bay Packers, Vincent Lombardi: "Winning isn't everything. It's the only thing." A number of sons and daughters of the 1990s feel their parents are like Coach Lombardi. If they don't score touchdowns in school, at camp, or in athletics, they will be utter failures as human beings.

Thousands of times I have heard children and teenagers say, "If I don't achieve what I know my parents want from me, they'll hate me and maybe even throw me out of the house." Paradoxically it is this attitude that leads to failure, because the youngster feels he is not loved for just being.

Depending on the way parents were brought up—either lovingly or hatefully—they help their children to develop either winning or losing scripts. When parents as children were pressured to achieve but in many ways felt like losers, they unwittingly but systematically train their children to feel incompetent in whatever they attempt.

In *Taking Chances: The Psychology of Losers,* Dr. Robert Lewis, discussing parents who promote failures and who feel like losers, says: "Their offspring will continually be reminded of their loser's role by admonitions such as 'Can't you ever learn to do something right?' 'Must you be so slow?' 'Here, let me do it for you.' 'You'll never learn—you're driving me crazy!' "

Many parents who take part in raising their children to become failures write the scripts that govern the drama produced. Children resemble the dreams of their parents.

The dreamer writes the script but wakes up saying, "What a horrible nightmare!" and does not recognize that he organized the entire action of the dream. Similarly, parents may be exasperated with their inhibited or angry, rebellious child but fail to recognize that they extended rewards and punishments to the child for acting in a certain way.

When parents talk about their children, they are always, without realizing it, talking about themselves. I have learned that the presentation of a child's problem by a mother or father constitutes a confession about themselves as a parent. When a mother or father tells me his or her child does not respond to limits, I know the parent is having difficulty setting limits and needs my help in understanding what his conflicts or inhibitions are all about. When a parent asks for my help in "straightening out" a child who is undergoing sexual difficulties or is seeking information about sex, it follows that the parent has sexual anxieties he has consciously or unconsciously conveyed to his child. If a parent tells me his child is lonely, in one way or another the parent is talking of his own difficulties in close relationships.

Because the child's problems are so intimately connected with his parents, when I work with mothers and fathers I try to help them unearth their own emotional investment in helping the child emerge in the manner they unconsciously arranged. A child is very sensitive to every word, every movement, every subtle look, whether it be of love or hate, that exists in the parent. Without realizing it, parents are constantly rewarding and punishing their children and in many ways moulding the type of human being that emerges—for better or for worse.

Several years ago I worked with a minister whose son had been convicted of stealing cars. It was, of course, humiliating and acutely embarrassing for the minister, who preached honesty, kindness and thoughtfulness of others, to learn his son had turned thief. But after working with my minister client for a few months, I became aware of the unconscious excitement he derived as he thought of his son's thefts. His sessions with me became dramatic reports of his son's criminal activities. Vicariously, although very secretly, my client was enjoying some rebellion within himself—activity his life-style obviously did not sanction.

When he became aware of the resentment he felt about "always having to live an uptight existence and be perfect in word, thought, and deed," he could understand how he participated in the forbidden activity he overtly condemned. In some unconscious way he had given his son permission to steal the cars.

Children and teenagers who act out sexually or in destructive or self-destructive ways are often subtly aided and abetted in these acts by parents. One of the best ways parents can help their children resolve learning difficulties, behavior problems, or lack of cooperation is to ask themselves "What secret satisfaction do I get when I think of my child behaving in this way?" Children copy their parents, both overtly and covertly, in more ways than we can imagine. Who else can the children learn from? The parent is their guide, their mentor, their role model—he can either make or break them, psychologically speaking.

Invariably the child who rebels, like the minister's son, gives the parent some vicarious pleasure. For example, the teenage girl who becomes pregnant and lets her parents know of this in one way or another, is cooperating with one or both of her parents' wishes.

When I interviewed Margaret, a sixteen-year-old who had become pregnant though unmarried, even as she showed anxiety and guilt, I realized her pregnancy had brought Margaret and her mother closer together than they had ever been. When I interviewed the mother, she confessed, "When I was a teenager sex was forbidden, talking about it was a crime. In my family you'd have to say it didn't exist. I must tell you, Doctor, that when I see Margaret pregnant, I feel a certain satisfaction because I know I have not deprived *her* of a sexual life."

There are many Margarets and many ministers' sons who are not able to handle life's regular tasks because they are encouraged unwittingly by parents to repair some defect of the parents' past. Whenever parents observe that their child is not coping well with life, they need to review the past of one or both of them.

The Child Within the Parent

Although there is much more to be learned about how we can improve parent-child relationships, we can say unequivocally that all parents recapitulate their childhood and teenage years as they live through the agonies and ecstasies of their child's development. When a baby is born and fed the parents, singly or together, relive that period in their childhood. If they experienced their early nurturing as loving and caring, they will treat their child as they themselves were treated. But many parents are not so fortunate; they may in childhood have experienced an absent or depressed mother or father. Trying to fill the void they suffered, they may hover over their child, who then becomes restless, fidgety, and irritable.

Sometimes, sensing their infant is getting the tender loving care they never received, they may become jealous and angry without knowing why. Many mothers or fathers who have consulted me and my colleagues are overwhelmed, angry, and depressed as they unconsciously relive their infantile past. After we help them understand their hurt and anger they are usually much more loving and relaxed with their child.

A woman who as a baby was weaned from the breast or the bottle with warmth of feeling and careful attention will probably be able to do the same with her child. A woman who notices that weaning is not working well should discuss with her spouse or some other friendly listener what she thinks took place when she was weaned. The exact facts are less important than what the mother *feels* took place.

Toilet training, living through the "terrible two's," childhood sexual curiosity, attending school, making friends, dating, and finally leaving home for college or a place in the world of work—these are tasks almost every boy and girl must confront.

Each parent, with the aid of the marital partner, should review what took place in his or her childhood or adolescence that may be disruptive to their child. The more parents know about themselves, the more easily they can help their child mature.

When society in general can accept the truism that all parents hold within them their child of the past, we will become more understanding of a parent's difficulties. When parents are able to like themselves and each other they will not be inclined to inflict emotional harm on their children. They will more likely provide a loving atmosphere in which the child grows and gains in self-esteem.

Children who are loved and understood become free to enjoy their studies, their teachers, their classmates, and recreation of all kinds. This sets them on the road to a pleasurable future that will bring a minimum of failures.

CHAPTER 4

FAILING TO LEARN

Whether it is a nursery of tots, a kindergarten of young children, or a doctoral seminar of mature and sophisticated adults, every classroom houses students who fail. Thousands of boys and girls and young women and men in many educational environments are depressed and anxious, unable to master tasks before them.

Academic failure has very little to do with native intelligence, a fact not well understood. Inability to master educational tasks is caused in 90 percent of the cases by psychological conflicts about which both students and teachers possess little knowledge.

The Need to Trust Teachers

Those researchers of the learning process who emphasize concepts such as repetition, conditioned responses, and reinforcement often fail to understand that how any of us learn, whether it be the youngster in first grade or the doctoral student in graduate school, depends in many ways on our first teachers—our mothers and fathers.

If an infant is fed nourishing milk by a loving mother who smiles and empathizes with him, she helps create someone who is open to receiving knowledge of the world about him. Those who are knowledgeable about learning processes speak of a thirst for knowledge that becomes ingested and digested. They contend that a good teacher provides ample opportunities for feedback—showing the student how well he is assimilating knowledge and supporting him in assimilating more.

Whether a student can trust a teacher and take in what the teacher offers depends on the atmosphere in which the student was originally fed and psychologically nourished. Whether it be the mother, the father, the nurse, the grandparents, or whoever else may have been entrusted to care for the infant, if these caretakers enjoy nurturing and if they emotionally and physically feed the child in a relaxed atmosphere, they provide some of the necessary ingredients for academic success in later years.

Many a slow learner, many an inattentive listener, many a child called stupid, found his early caretaking "disgusting," impossible to "take in." The word *disgusting* comes from the Latin *gustare*, which means "to taste." If a teacher or the information of a course is experienced as disgusting, learning becomes distasteful, and the child will turn away from it.

Ellen, a graduate student of twenty-two, consulted me because she found her graduate work in psychology and education "most unappetizing." After she described her professors, I asked her to tell me about her seminars. She called them boring and confessed she often left a seminar feeling depressed and irritable.

In Ellen's case I had to decipher what it was about her graduate work that made it so unappetizing, inasmuch as she had been quite successful as a student throughout high school and college. When I asked what was so different about her graduate school experience from her previous experience as a student, she explained, "Until I attended graduate school I lived at home with my parents, but now I'm on my own in a city far from home and feel like an outcast."

As she spoke more openly of her separation from home, Ellen told me that when she was less than two, her mother fell ill. Ellen was then cared for by a nursemaid whom everybody described as "dull, ungiving, and not a bit stimulating." This was in contrast to Ellen's mother who, she thought, was "warm, outgoing, and fun."

Ellen and I discovered that her current separation from home rekindled memories of the very early separation from her mother. The "dull professors" in the master's program were to Ellen like the dull nursemaid of her past, "unstimulating and unappetizing," at a time she yearned to return to her mother.

When Ellen could talk freely about the days she felt uncared for, banished from home and mother, she was quickly able to regain interest enough to want to help relieve her misery and understand the causes of it. When she realized how she had distorted her current educational experience, she started to become interested in what her professors had to say.

There exists much variation among teachers at all levels of the educational ladder. Some are warm and stimulating, others are dull and boring, still others belligerent. An important part of understanding the failure to thrive in an educational environment is how the learner experiences his teacher.

Very often teachers of all kinds—swimming instructors, golf pros, clergymen—become to us replicas of figures of the past. This means we cannot take in the knowledge our current teachers wish to give us because we think of them as the ungiving caretakers of our early, sometimes miserable lives.

Many young and not-so-young students become nauseous during a lecture, seminar, or classroom project. One young woman told me that when a professor was talking away "about nothing," she wanted to "scream to the high heavens," as she put it, in boredom and anger at being forced to listen to words that meant nothing to her. She and other students like her experienced the professor as giving bad milk, which was difficult to ingest. As I worked with these students, encouraged them to face their resentments toward the teacher who reminded them of past caretakers, they slowly accepted this buried truth and in new awareness started to take part in the learning process.

Many times accidental factors occur in a youngster's early life, such as a mother or father's illness, an unexpected move, or the "premature" birth of a sibling. All children to some extent experience the birth of a sibling as premature. They feel displaced, and they frequently have to be weaned once more, in a sense, when a baby sister or brother is born. Some lose their appetite and feel like biting the hand that feeds them. Many children, many teenagers and many adults cannot learn in a group situation because they have to share the teacher—an experience like sharing their mother and father with a sibling. They feel they are now just a nobody, their former kingdom blown up.

Many failures in many educational settings are essentially bright students who experience their classmates as brothers and sisters standing in their way of receiving love and attention from the parental figure, the teacher. Such students are so angry with the teacher for imposing so many sibling rivals on them that they refuse to listen to or accept anything the teacher says. They are like angry children who feel so upset with their parents that they refuse to eat. Refusal to eat and refusal to learn are similar processes. Just as the angry child may punish his parents by refusing to eat, many students punish their teachers by refusing to learn.

Overachievers, on the other hand, punish themselves in that they drive themselves unmercifully to be the best and are never truly content with their achievements, even when they bring the temporary honor of being at the top of the class. Overachievers also resent the colleagues who begrudge them their achievements while racking up much lower marks.

The impact of sharing a teacher with symbolic siblings and of the resentment the latter induce is not sufficiently appreciated by most educators. Tom, a boy of thirteen, was referred to me because his parents felt he should be smarter than his below-average IQ score. The parents were correct; he was a very bright lad.

When he took his IQ tests he always sat among peers, but when I saw him alone and gave him a verbal IQ test, his score rose thirty points. This showed once again that certain people may thrive in a one-on-one atmosphere in which they feel parented but deteriorate in a group atmosphere where their peers are experienced as sadistic intruders.

Tom was the first-born of seven children. I encouraged him to talk about his feelings as the oldest child of such a large family. He willingly shared with me his deep longing to have his parents all to himself once in a while, apart from his brothers and sisters. Eventually he could understand that he felt like a nobody in a group situation with his teacher, believing that she, like his parents, did not know he existed. He was able to become more relaxed in the classroom when he realized that he no longer had to feel like the displaced oldest brother and that his teacher was not his overburdened parent who did not have enough time or energy for him.

Eric Erikson, the noted child psychologist, referred to the first period of life as the trust-mistrust period. During this short time, it is hoped, we learn to trust our caretakers. If a child cannot trust a teacher, he cannot learn. When we distrust a mentor, it is helpful to find out what in the caretaker or current teacher evokes memories of earlier caretakers. If we can share our former distrustful feelings with someone we trust, we feel more at ease with the one who furthers our learning process.

The Delicate Process of Learning

The learning process can be complicated. It involves more than just taking in new ideas. To learn requires a cooperative attitude between teacher and student, the two main actors on the educational stage. If they want to cooperate with each other, respect and like each other, learning can become a mutually enhancing experience.

Many students of all ages tend to equate the learning process with an earlier time in their lives when they felt submissive and subordinate to their caretakers. Many students *unconsciously* associate homework, study, and other activities where their cooperation is needed with being compelled to move their bowels or urinate for a parent.

Just as children can be constipated because they harbor spiteful feelings toward parents or others, there are students who cannot perform educational tasks because they feel they are arbitrarily submitting to overdemanding parental figures. Intellectual constipation is probably as prevalent as physical constipation.

Why is it so important, and sometimes so difficult, to toilet train an infant? For one thing, when toilet training starts, usually by the age of two, the infant has spent two years feeling free to urinate whenever he wants. How easily he may be toilet-trained depends on how free his parents allow him to be. If they push him or scream at him when he does not control urination, he may become scared or angry. If, however, his parents are understanding, he will slowly learn to urinate only in the toilet. Unfortunately, in some of the poorer areas of our country children have been battered because they refused to learn to control their urination or bowel movements. The assailants are usually the parents, who unconsciously or consciously remember how cruelly their parents treated them at a similar time in their growth.

When children have to hold themselves in check prematurely or control themselves in an atmosphere of tension and resentment, they are not going to cooperate readily with future teachers, no matter what the area of knowledge.

I treated Harvey, a nine-year-old boy who came for help because he could not read, although he was very intelligent. Harvey's parents told me (without realizing it) that he had been brought up in a very exacting atmosphere. He was weaned from the bottle at three months of age and toilet-trained at six months, which is far too early. Although Harvey complied with his parents' edicts, understandably he was often consumed with rage toward them because of the premature excessive demands on his mind and body.

I discovered that Harvey was compliant on the surface but inwardly fuming. I realized that, though not openly rebellious, he was bent on spiting his demanding parents by refusing to read. He knew they desperately wanted him to learn to read, just as they had fervently wanted to wean him and toilet train him. Though Harvey appeared to be trying to cooperate in learning to read, he subtly fought this act all the way.

Harvey did very well in play therapy. He enjoyed competitive games such as cards and checkers. He also had a strong wish to cheat, to "break the rules." Because I was his therapist and wished to empathize with his wish to break rules, I encouraged him to cheat. I too cheated at cards and checkers, as if I approved of it.

Harvey had a ball as I helped him break the rules, in contrast to his parents, who insisted on strict conformity. He began to like and trust me, looked forward to our sessions where we would both break the rules. I became a parental figure who did not insist on obedience to arbitrary rules but, to the contrary, helped him by approving his disobedient behavior because of harsh rules too early in life. This allowed him to feel he could be loved without going through harsh, premature performances for a pressuring audience—his parents.

He worked steadily with me for six months, and although his parents were shocked at his changes, such as cheating at checkers, they were gratified when he started to became interested in his academic pursuits.

Very often the rebellious, belligerent students, whether toddlers, teenagers, or graduate students, defy the educational establishment because they experience their mentors as making unreasonable demands. Young children who "mess up" by spilling milk or hot chocolate, or dropping and breaking glasses, or older students who make belligerent remarks about their teachers, are contemptuously sneering at them and their orders.

To learn, a pupil must possess the freedom to feel curious and to be curious. Those students who enjoy learning have been permitted to be curious as children and to have their curiosity satisfied. Many parents unfortunately respond to curious children with the retort, "Curiosity killed the cat," implying that curiosity is something that leads to death. What is the truth of the matter?

Curiosity begins very early in life, perhaps in the womb, and reaches a new height by the time the child is three or four. It is then that the youngster becomes aware of sexual differences and shows great curiosity about them. He is eager to know where babies come from and to learn the differences between the male and female anatomy. He becomes curious about sexual intercourse.

If parents and other caretakers believe this kind of curiosity is taboo, the child is forced to squelch his curiosity, knowing it will get him into trouble. Above all, he very much needs his parents' love and approval at this time and worries about their abandoning him—a child's deepest fear.

I have found that when the sexual misconceptions of children, teenagers, and adults are aired and discussed and when their fears of sexual fantasies are expressed verbally, in almost every case their ability to learn becomes greatly accelerated. It is as though new energy for learning that previously was used to repress dangerous feelings about sex is now released in the interest of different pursuits.

A six-year-old boy, Ivan, felt deeply depressed and refused to learn. As I worked with him in play therapy, he slowly became interested in naked dolls. He started to reveal to me his lack of clarity about sexual differences and the birth process. When I answered his questions, corrected his misconceptions, and did so in a relaxed manner, his learning improved dramatically. Even more important was helping his parents realize that curiosity, particularly sexual curiosity, is a creative, natural feeling. I reviewed with them how their own old-fashioned parents had sometimes made sex unspeakable and showed them how they were unwittingly recapitulating their puritanical past with their son. As, in effect, I gave them permission to be sexual people and also to relate to the child in each of them that was afraid to admit sexual curiosity, they could do the same with Ivan.

Most of us understand that if children are not lovingly nurtured and not given honest answers to their questions, they will respond to most adults with resentment, revenge, and revulsion. They will strive to defeat their mentors' efforts to teach them, whether they are teachers in a classroom or authors of their textbooks.

There are, however, more subtle ways in which students express their antipathy toward learning. Many youngsters, as well as teenagers and adults, become sleepy, sick, or bored during a learning situation. Often they appear superficially co-operative as they silently fight learning. It would appear that most academic failures are expressed in this manner—subtly and indirectly through tiredness, illness, boredom, or depression. Why is this so?

In the process of growing up, most children much of the time do not feel safe enough to question parental edicts or secure enough to voice their resentments. Whether parental edicts in their minds are unwanted impositions or are actually unfair, most children, because of their small size, vulnerability, and intense need for their parents' love, squelch their anger, repress their hateful fantasies, and try to submit to their parents' orders. Frequently, the more youngsters feel the need to repress their anger, the stronger the anger becomes.

When it is repressed, rebellion takes the form of headaches, phobias, compulsions, and other symptoms. The child riddled with symptoms cannot fully learn because his energy and attention are focused on his aches and pains.

Parents, teachers, and even guidance instructors do not always realize that the seemingly obedient child who appears to be trying to conform and to cooperate but cannot learn because he or she is suffering from a stomachache or headache is really an angry, frightened child, covertly fighting the process of learning.

I worked with a nine-year-old girl, Sarah, well liked by her teachers and peers. She was described as cooperative and pleasant but often ill from headaches and backaches that forced her to stay home. Sarah's IQ test scores revealed high intelligence, yet she fell far behind in reading, writing, and in virtually every other phase of learning.

As I worked with her and her parents, I discovered that Sarah, the oldest child in the family, with a brother two years younger and a sister three years younger, was loved and appreciated at home only when she worked diligently. In other words, she felt loved if she persisted in presenting herself as a hardworking, productive, cooperative girl. Sarah's parents did not encourage her to play or admire and praise her when she enjoyed herself in pursuits of her own choosing, including doing nothing at times, as most of us like to do. Because Sarah did not feel free to protest the unfair way her parents treated her she could express her anger and pain only through bodily symptoms.

School to her was a torture chamber in which she felt

pressured to achieve. But, as at home, she could not permit herself to put into words how angry she felt. Instead, she expressed herself through her physical symptoms and fought learning in a subtle but real way.

Not only children but many teenagers and adults cannot permit themselves consciously to feel their resentment toward authorities and, instead, tune out of the learning process. Many times teenagers or adults who cannot understand the content of a particular article or book, or whose minds wander while they read, are unaware of the fight they are waging with the author. It may be an honest disagreement or genuine resentment at what the author says. Or the author may be unwittingly ascribed the qualities of an arbitrary parent whom the teenager or adult experiences as a punitive taskmaster.

All of us, children and adults, probably could learn more and master more if we were more closely in touch with how we feel toward the teacher, whether a dead author or someone to whom we are currently relating. How much we learn and how much we retain is greatly influenced by how we feel toward the one from whom we learn. Sometimes we distort the teacher when we make her or him a mean mommy or daddy from our past. Sometimes the teacher actually is a provocative person toward whom we should allow ourselves to feel honest anger. If we hold back from expressing what we feel is threatening or belligerent, our energy becomes destructively used as we quickly assign it to the deeper levels of our mind. We then have less energy for learning as we use it to suppress the rage we feel.

Learning is much like a feeding process. If we resent the one who feeds us, the food cannot be easily ingested nor digested. Learning can also be viewed as a cooperative venture, similar in many ways to making love. If our partner upsets us we cannot enjoy the lovemaking. Similarly, in learning, if our partner during the learning situation appears insensitive, pressuring, or intrusive, we cannot easily learn and do not enjoy the experience.

When Learning Is a Pleasure

To understand the more subtle forms academic failure can take, we need to look at what psychologists refer to as the school phobia. When a youngster suffers such a phobia he feels terrified of going to school. Often he may vomit on the way, or in the classroom. He may appear terrified of his teacher or of his peers. Sometimes this school-phobic youngster may reveal that he is afraid to cross the street alone or is frightened of the neighborhood bullies.

It is not sufficiently understood that the school-phobic youngster's fear of school has little to do with school per se, with the class, or with what he has learned or not learned. Rather, he feels upset because he cannot separate peacefully from his parents. If they are out of sight he becomes frantic. He wonders if they are alive or if they have fallen sick; he imagines dreadful things happening to them. This is the child who wails in deep anguish, "I want my mommy!" He feels that if he does not have her at hand he will not survive.

Why is he so convinced he will die without the presence of his mother? The reason is that the child, without being aware of it, harbors deep resentment toward a mother he feels does not love him. Unconsciously he wishes her dead, but of course he finds this horrendous idea unacceptable.

The reasons he wishes her to disappear from the earth

vary from child to child. One child may be furious with his mother for staying home with a younger sibling whom, he is convinced, she loves more than him, as he is forced to go to school with strangers surrounding him all day. Another child may sense a mother's unconscious rejection and feel angry that his mother wants him out of the house. There is also the child who has been so indulged and so excessively infantilized that to be expected to appear independent is experienced as a hard slap in the face. He, too, fights separation. Such a child, originally treated like a prince, resists being part of a group where he does not stand out as somebody special.

The school-phobic youngster, regardless of his home situation, is terrified to leave home. When he cannot *see* his mother, father, or siblings, he starts to wonder if they are still alive and well. Actually, he secretly wishes them to be not so alive and not so well; he secretly wishes them dead.

Since he cannot tolerate such destructive thoughts, he becomes phobic about school. We know that separation anxiety is the crucial issue with the school-phobic child because when his mother accompanies him to school and sits beside him in the classroom or at least within sight, his symptoms diminish and he is free to concentrate. Seeing his mother in class, the child is reassured that he has not killed her—she is alive and well.

Other youngsters are unable to separate from their parents and attend school because the parents are not ready to let the child out of their sight. In my work with children suffering from school phobia, I found that the child who resists going to school has either one or two parents who are emotionally reluctant to release him from the house.

What we have said about school-phobic youngsters is also applicable to high school students, college students, even graduate students. They are not exempt from separation anxiety. I recall working with a college freshman, Sam, who had achieved excellent grades in high school but was about to flunk out of a prominent university in New York City.

I learned from Sam as he discussed his homesickness that he felt deep resentment toward his parents, who "forced me to leave our lovely town in Vermont to come to this ghastly city of New York," as he put it. Further discussion revealed that he experienced attending college as being premature; he had been forced to become independent too swiftly. Yet he could not permit himself to feel the hurt and disappointment, as well as the fury, caused by his parents who "threw me out and made me come to this dirty city."

I empathized with Sam's hurt and his anger, and I encouraged him to talk about earlier hurts and angers during his life with his parents. His ability to master his work grew by leaps and bounds as he was permitted to be himself with me. Sam taught me what is probably the most important lesson as to why children, teenagers, and adults become academic failures. The failures occur because the children, teenagers, and adults are not allowed by parents and others to be themselves. All of us are far more able to learn when we are accepted for who we are and when we can accept our own feelings, whatever they may be. The able learner is one who feels accepted by his mentors and can feel free to be himself with his own unique emotional reactions.

A frequent visitor to a mental health professional is the high school or college teenager who has been a competent student but seems suddenly no longer able to cope with his or her schoolwork. While there are many reasons to account for this failure, one major factor is often overlooked—the intensity of a young person's sexual conflicts.

During the teenage years the sexual drive reaches its highest peak. Many young people feel guilty and anxious as they experience strong fantasies that show their wishes to gratify themselves sexually. If they have been reared in a home or community where sexuality is not accepted as a fact of life, they start to feel like perverts or lunatics because of the strange new feelings that possess body and mind.

To ward off the discomfort that a burgeoning sexuality evokes and to try to modify a self-image that appears tarnished when they feel sexually stimulated, many young people expend considerable energy trying to become celibates or crusaders against vice. As we have pointed out, the young person who expends a great deal of mental energy trying to suppress a natural feeling or wish cannot concentrate on academic obligations. A seventeen-year-old boy or girl who feels guilty about masturbating and then works hard to suppress such a natural desire has less mental energy available to concentrate on algebra or English literature. When I have helped young people overcome some of their guilt about sexual fantasies and accept the fact that feeling sexual is being human, their academic work has improved dramatically.

Another word should be said about sexuality during the teenage years and its impact on learning. Young people inevitably possess homosexual fantasies. If parents and other important authorities do not recognize that homosexual fantasies are par for the course, particularly during adolescence, these young people will feel very guilty and somewhat like freaks; they are not free to concentrate on learning if plagued with thoughts about how aberrant they are.

Although it is more acceptable in the 1990s than ever

before, many of us still cannot accept the biological and psychological truism that there exists in all of us wishes and fantasies to achieve sexual closeness with both sexes. Most of us have had close relationships with both a mother and a father, often too, with a sister or brother. The yearning for intimate physical contact with both sexes starts fairly early in life—about three or four years of age—and continues indefinitely. The good learner, no matter how old, is the one who accepts all of the elements that go into being human.

Another of the most pressing factors leading to academic failure are high expectations. The child, the teenager, or the adult who feels pressured to produce at a superlative level is probably going to fail to meet them—and perhaps fail altogether.

In my work with doctoral candidates unable to complete their dissertation and, in many cases, even to start one, I discovered that one reason is that they felt they had to write the great American novel. When I convinced them that a doctoral dissertation is merely an extended term paper, they could complete it.

What has been said of doctoral students applies to nursery school toddlers. If they feel pressured to accomplish tasks that are literally and figuratively over their heads, they are likely to fail.

The competitive culture in which we live does not lead us to consider learning a pleasure. More often it is used to "beat out" rivals and to achieve status. Our schools, from kindergarten to graduate school, overemphasize competition and status. They give little attention to providing an atmosphere in which learning, like eating food and having sex, can be a deep pleasure.

If someone competes at the dinner table or the restaurant to show how fast he can eat or how great a gourmet he is, he does not truly enjoy his food. If the emphasis is on competition as to who has the more satisfying sex life, this will interfere with sexual pleasure. The sense of being pressured in any situation will interfere with our pleasure and contribute to our failure.

Academic failure is all too often viewed as immoral and as evidence of stupidity, rather than as a sign of conflict and human suffering. When the emphasis in learning is shifted from stiff competition to pleasure, there will be fewer academic failures.

Even those students in elementary schools, high schools, and college who do not fail, who are often at the top of their class, may be psychological failures. They believe they cannot like themselves unless they are in the top position. Such students may become very depressed, even shattered at times. To enjoy the learning process, we must feel loved and must love ourselves, our mentors, and our peers.

CHAPTER 5

FAILING AT WORK

Roy, fifty-six years old, tall and well dressed, with a warm, outgoing manner, walked into my office for a consultation. He slowly sat down in the patient's comfortable chair, then explained, "You see, Doc, the reason I'm here is because I've been in eleven different businesses over the last thirteen years."

He laughed nervously, adding, not in shame but almost as a boast, "That's almost one business a year."

He then told of an exciting venture the year before in which he felt "on top of the world," only to watch the business soon plunge into disaster. He sighed, saying in a tone of resignation, "I've been a millionaire several times and a pauper in debt several times. I either fly high or I'm on my ass."

He blamed his failures on the economy, occasionally on business partners that he had selected or on the industry he chose. He concluded, "But most of the time I just think it's been bad luck."

His ventures included electronics, computers, horticulture, clothing, and furniture. Each time he started off with confidence, excited at the thought of success. But then he found himself bored with the work, irritated with his partners, upset with his customers or clients. Eventually he fought a deep depression over his failures.

"I'm never sure which comes first, the depression or the business reversal," he complained. "Maybe they both arrive at once."

As I learned more about Roy I discovered that what had happened to him in business also occurred in other areas of his life. He had married three times, each time beginning with a passionate love affair, an exciting honeymoon, and an elated feeling during the first six months of marriage. But after this he tumbled downhill, psychologically speaking, as he became irritable with his wife and bored with the relationship. Each marriage ended after four or five years.

A similar trend of initial excitement followed by depression and boredom marked his friendships, his hobbies, and even his relationships with his two daughters. Early in his therapy, while Ray was starting to understand that what happened to him in business also took place in his doomed love relationships and friendships, it began to dawn on him that the theme of riding high, then plunging to the hard ground, permeated his life style. He discovered something that frequently eludes men and women who fail in business—they themselves play a large role in the failure, unwittingly contributing to it in more ways than they realize.

Luck certainly is a variable, and the economy does have its upturns and downturns. Partners, employees, and clients can be destructive and difficult. But in the dozens of men and women who have consulted me about business failures I have always found that the person who experiences the failure has a strong tendency, although unwittingly, to sabotage his own success.

I soon realized that Roy possessed an avid yearning for excitement and adventure but could not accept the drudgery and hard work inevitable in any business, profession, or vocation. Just as he could not tolerate anything but complete bliss in each of his three marriages, he could not accept the day-to-day routine and inevitable frustrations that exist in business—as well as in marriage.

Like the many men and women who fail in love and work, Roy was indignant when I questioned him about his strong need to be on a constant "high." Just as he felt his wives should provide him with perennial excitement, he believed his business partners should. It was painful for Roy to recognize, as it is for most men and women who fail at work, that every job requires discipline, dedication, and frustration. Bliss, whether it is in marriage or work, is a momentary phenomenon. Roy was looking for perpetual bliss, a totally unrealistic and unattainable state of human existence.

Every one of us has a desire for eternal bliss. We all wish to be applauded constantly, to feel the excitement of being a winner as often as possible, if not all the time. But the mature person, the realistic person, recognizes and accepts that though bliss is a magnificent, joyous state of mind, it does not endure indefinitely. Reality has a way of asserting itself.

The Need for Discipline and Dedication

Those who seek perpetual bliss, as Roy did, are really refusing to become adult, which involves facing many unpleasant, frustrating moments. An adult does not expect to be always warmly held at the breast; the nearest feeling to this is a tender hug by a loved one or perhaps a coffee break with congenial comrades.

A responsive, sympathetic comment or an outstanding success stimulates us and should be enjoyed. But Roy, like many men and women, lived in a perpetual rage because all of his businesses eventually required something besides adventure and excitement. He could not face the reality that he had to engage in hard, disciplined work to make a go of it.

In his book, *Staying the Course: The Emotional and Social Lives of Men Who Do Well at Work,* Dr. Robert Weiss points out that men who are successful in their work and achieve a place in society that most of us consider satisfactory have worked hard to fashion such lives for themselves, for their families, for their business associates. They are staying the course.

Many writers have explored the reasons why someone becomes an outstanding, creative person, fewer have pointed out an essential ingredient in all successful work—consistent discipline and dedication. Many men and women view the successful businessman, the best-selling author, the dramatist who receives rave reviews, as a person who is just fortunate, who has been blessed by good luck. But Einstein worked diligently; Freud saw patients for ten hours every day, then wrote his important books into the early morning hours. Newton, Galileo, Hemingway, and Arthur Miller were all dedicated workers.

Many of us ascribe to successful people our own childish wishes. In our minds they were loved and adored by everyone, seldom had to work hard, if at all, and escaped frustration.

Just as there are men and women who go from one love

affair to another, tiring quickly of the relationship when excitement, romance, and adventurous feelings begin to ebb, so too there are many who go from business to business, job to job, expecting it to be a Garden of Eden or that elusive Paradise.

Two of the essential ingredients of success in business or in any line of work are to take initiative and absorb frustration. Only an adult can accept this. Many men and women who fail at work are preoccupied with keeping themselves indulged children.

Recently a man in his early forties, Michael, a free-lance writer who had not made much money in the past few years, arrived at my office. Living on loans from friends and family, he felt bitter because he could not sell his novels, plays, or poems. He was very depressed, thinking his life was a complete failure. He was also angry with friends who were asking him to return the borrowed money. He inquired sarcastically, "How can I pay them back when no one is knocking at my door wanting what I write?"

Michael felt that the world should take care of him, buy his written projects, give him both monetary and psychological rewards simply because he deserved them. As he started to explore his early life, I learned that he was the oldest child of three, adored by his mother and father, who considered him exceptional. His teachers were convinced he was an outstanding pupil. Although talented, unfortunately he had acquired the belief that he was a prince and therefore entitled to the privileges and pleasures of royalty.

Michael felt that others should take care of him. Many men and women cannot stay the course, have never been helped to accept the reality that success requires, the taking on and the enduring of many frustrations as they move ahead. Just as husbands and wives who do not expect perfection from each other enjoy marriage more, those who accept some of the drudgery of work are in a much better position to extract some of the pleasures from it.

Eventually Michael started to accept the demands, relinquished his princely role, and settled down to earn a living on Wall Street. He had been able to face in his sessions with me his earlier life of unreal expectations and start facing the reality that he would, at times, have to work hard to achieve lasting success.

Facing Our Resentments and Jealousies

One of the difficulties both Roy and Michael revealed in therapy was the need to be on center stage at all times. Roy told me that as long as he was in charge of a project he felt happy and got the work done. But if someone else took the limelight, Roy became angry and competitive, and he either engaged in arguments or withdrew as the project failed. Michael pointed out that when one of his artistic creations was rejected, he felt depressed and angry for weeks. And he felt furious with those who had achieved fame and fortune.

Whether we are board chairmen, secretaries, authors, or employees on the assembly line, work requires cooperation with others, no matter if the latter be supervisors or subordinates, colleagues or clients. If we must occupy center stage constantly, must be the star performer at all times, at work or anywhere else, we are doomed to failure.

Unfortunately those who do not do well in the workplace and who oppose others do not realize that they *seek* fights. They have a tendency to make the boss into the tyrannical father or overprotective mother of the past.

They regularly feel competitive with colleagues and try to surpass them as they tried to surpass their siblings.

Pauline, a forty-two-year-old woman with a supervisory job in a social agency, asked for help because she felt very depressed. Another younger woman who had worked at the agency for a shorter period of time had been promoted to a job above Pauline's, with more status and a higher salary. To Pauline, this was the injustice of the century. "The idea that somebody with less experience is getting ahead of me is unbelievable!" she wailed at one session.

While no one likes to be surpassed, particularly by someone we feel possesses less talent and less experience, life is not always fair and the most appropriate persons are not always treated best. We all have a right to feel anger and hurt when we are actually discriminated against at work or anywhere else. But when the anger and hurt refuse to dissipate so that we cannot concentrate on the tasks at hand, as was true of Pauline, we need to look inward.

Pauline discovered much about herself that contributed heavily to her agitated depression. The elder of two sisters, she grew up to see Mary receive from both parents higher praise and more expensive clothes. While some of this discrimination was probably distorted in her mind, because each child wishes to be the favorite every moment of the day and night, Pauline never lost the deep conviction that Mary was always favored.

The rage she felt toward her parents had never been discharged at them. Rather, she tended to express it at work, just as when she was younger she unleashed it at college through her friends. Many who feel they are held in disfavor by parents restrain themselves from raging at the source of their anger but act it out in the workplace or in social situations.

When we experience rejection we tend to view the rejection as character assassination, as we question our own worth. Constantly reliving her rivalry with her sister, Pauline felt inferior to every one of her peers in each situation, yet she tried hard to convince herself and others that she was as loved and as worthy of love as Mary.

I have found that when men and women are excessively competitive on the job with peers, they are often reenacting fights from the past with brothers and sisters. They need help in realizing that if their brothers or sisters were favored, in reality or just in their imagination, they do not have to conclude and should not conclude they are inferior beings, unlovable and unworthy.

Most of us who collect injustices, however legitimate, feel weak and vulnerable and do not like ourselves. Rather than face why we do not like ourselves, we feel in disfavor—due to the way our parents may have looked at us at times—and attack the system, the boss or the union.

If we feel we are frequently discriminated against, we should face the fact that we do not like ourselves sufficiently and that we are rejecting ourselves the way we felt rejected as a child. In this day and age rivalry between peers and resentment toward bosses is so prevalent that many employers provide opportunities to discuss these issues openly and directly. Rivalry, when discussed openly and understood to be present in the mind and heart of all of us, results in a reduction of it in day-to-day behavior. When we realize that everyone feels a sense of rivalry much of the time, we no longer have to feel guilty.

The mature and successful adult is one who recognizes that competition and resentment are par for the course of work and play. The mature person does not damn his colleagues and bosses constantly. He faces his own resentments, jealousies, and competitiveness; he realizes he has turned figures in the present to ghosts of the past; and then he is able to move on to face reality, heartbreaking as it is at times.

Accepting the Inner and Outer Self

As we have seen, one failure may lead to another, and often it is difficult to know what sets off a whole cluster of sequential failures. Several years ago Jerry, thirty-nine years old, arrived at my office for psychotherapy. He possessed several of what we call presenting problems. He drank to excess on many occasions, often felt depressed, and got into serious marital fights after which he and his wife did not speak to each other for weeks at a time.

To add insult to injury Jerry was frequently impotent sexually, and even when he tried to have sex with a woman other than his wife he proved to be a failure.

As I worked with Jerry I learned he had never been able to stay in one job or business for more than two years. He would find himself in power struggles with subordinates, peers, and superiors. As he put it, "I seem always to be in a fight. I rarely get along with anybody."

Like many other men, Jerry relived in the arena of work family squabbles from childhood. He had originally lived through a tempestuous relationship with an authoritarian, punitive father and competed actively with two brothers, one older, one younger. At work Jerry constantly felt threatened, as if he were home again and had to fight for his psychic survival.

The only way he could win a battle was by leaving the job. He told me that many times as a boy he had felt like running away from home "to spite the whole family." On the job he felt momentary pleasure each time he abandoned the "boss father" and his peers, who were, in his mind, "nasty brothers."

When Jerry quit jobs he would feel morose, like a son or brother who had abandoned his family. Then guilt would take over. Jerry shared with me the secret that even when he found himself in the middle of an altercation at work, he wanted to make up with his business associates, as he had earlier with his brothers and father.

The strong conflict between Jerry's wish to fight bosses and peers and the hunger to get along with them made him feel perpetually depressed and anxious. To try to dissipate his tensions he would take a drink. One drink led to another and, without realizing it, he became an alcoholic.

His alcoholism interfered with his sexual potency, and he then felt more bereft as his wife became increasingly dissatisfied with him. The vicious cycle kept recurring until I could help him understand that at work he was fighting futile battles which, in the end, were self-destructive.

When a psychotherapist sees someone like Jerry it is difficult for a while to understand why he is so upset and why he is plagued by so many problems. Jerry was not only suffering from marital and sexual conflicts; he was also depressed, irritable, and alcoholic. However, all these problems were triggered by his strong, although unconscious desire to turn the job situation into a boxing arena in which he slugged it out with a father figure and male siblings.

Alcoholism, depression, and sexual difficulties may all be symptoms of dissatisfaction with the job. You can tell an alcoholic to take all the necessary steps Alcoholic Anonymous prescribes, but he will achieve only limited results unless he faces his battles on the job. Similarly, you can prescribe and proscribe all kinds of techniques to a man or woman beset by sexual problems, but if the competitive and revengeful fantasies on the job are not faced, all the proposed sexual techniques will have limited impact.

Often when a man or woman comes to me for marital counseling, I soon realize that their marriages can be improved if they feel more accepting of themselves and fulfilled in their jobs. While not every marital or sexual problem evolves from dissatisfaction at work or from lack of fulfillment on the job, many, perhaps most, adults value themselves on the basis of how they achieve on the job front. And even though marital and parent-child conflicts stem from many sources, it is amazing how much better people feel and function in many areas of living when they feel happy in work.

For many years I was consultant to a county department of public welfare in Bergen County, New Jersey, where I live. Every week social workers would bring me cases of disorganized families where the parents eternally bickered with each other and with their children and where there was only limited emotional gratification for family members. I found almost always that when the father, and often the mother, began to work at something he or she at least partially enjoyed, many family conflicts greatly diminished.

What we do for a living affects our self-image deeply. If we value our work and if others value us for it we tend to like ourselves more. As we like ourselves, we feel warmer and more loving toward others. A sequence evolves in which, just as one failure leads to another, success breeds success. The man or woman happy in work is more likely to be happier and more loving in all other dimensions of living.

Although what we do for a living can enrich our self-esteem and enhance our image, it can also lead to many problems. We live in a society that is very status-conscious. A professional person is accorded higher status than the nonprofessional. Consequently, many parents exert great pressure on their children to aspire to the favored positions.

Perhaps one of the most frequent questions asked of a youngster is, "What do you want to be when you grow up?" Most young people know the correct answers; they describe a position that they perceive has high status, such as doctor, dentist, lawyer, engineer. I have yet to hear a boy or girl tell me he or she looks forward to being no one special.

The great pressure placed on children to aspire to certain positions regardless of their own wishes, preferences, and talents often leads to disaster. Children want to please their parents and obey their mandates even if they do not find the mandates acceptable. In my practice I have met many professional men and women who feel miserable because they are engaged in work they do not really like, for they still obey the voices of parents or other important figures, such as grandparents or teachers who once pressured them to seek what the older person wished.

If parents truly love their child and want him to like himself, they will give him the freedom to act on his own preferences, not squelch his inclinations and choices. I am often asked, "Do children really *know* what they want to be?"

If parents observe children they will note that the growing child begins to show interest and lack of interests, things he will adore and things he will abhor. If a child does not like music, comparative anatomy, or biology, why pressure him to like it just because it has status value? Or if a child enjoys playing with stamps or saving baseball cards, why squelch his interest even if these activities do not have immense status value? Children may not be able to say with conviction, "I want to be a stamp collector when I grow up," but they do give many hints as to what they really want to do.

The mature, loving parent encourages his son's or daughter's preference even if it is not his own. He can accept his youngster's dislike of activities that he enjoys, such as visiting museums, playing golf, or haunting the football stands from autumn through February.

In choosing an occupation, not only are the child's natural talents and spontaneous likes and dislikes crucial elements but of equal importance is the relationship that exists between parent and child. Many children *avoid* certain occupations and professions because their parents work in them. Other children get involved in certain occupations and professions because their parents *are* in them.

This does not imply that a child who chooses a profession or occupation that is the same as his parent's loves his parent, nor does it imply that if a child chooses something different he hates his parent. The issue is a complex one. Many sons and daughters are revolted by the profession or occupation of their parents because they feel revulsion toward the parents, whereas other children, not out of pressure, not out of compulsion, but out of love choose the line of work held by a loving mother or father, wanting to identify with their parents, be close to them, carry on the family tradition. What is crucial is that young and not so young people should be urged to work in professions and vocations they enjoy. If they feel compelled to work in a specific environment by parents or other significant persons in their lives, they will be doomed to failure.

As Marsha Sinetar points out in her book *Do What You Love: The Money Will Follow,* all of us have a better chance of making a good living if we work at what we love. We heartily agree with this belief because we have seen many men and women, in high-paying jobs they hate, who fall sick, are often absent from work, and are forced to give a large part of their income to physicians and psychotherapists.

In a chapter titled "What Price Success?" in *Behind the Couch* I wrote about the case of a prominent physician who had made a fortune but felt deeply unhappy in his work. Even though his parents were dead he was still trying to secure their love, often remembering wistfully how proudly they referred to him as "my son, the doctor."

This patient, Dr. Epstein, after two years of work with me, decided to give up his hated practice of medicine in New York and to do something he had wanted to do since a child—open a hot-dog stand in San Francisco, where he was born.

When engaged in the work he enjoyed at the place he recalled as so beautiful, his self-confidence grew by leaps and bounds. Not only did his relationship with his wife and children dramatically shift from irritability to devotion and love but a series of psychosomatic complaints, including headaches, insomnia, and gastrointestinal pains, vanished.

While Dr. Epstein never made quite the amount of money in the hot-dog business that he made in medicine, in psychic income he felt as if he were a multimillionaire.

Enjoying the Pleasure of Work

Just as aspiring to status can wreck job satisfaction, which in turn can wreck marriages, friendships, and a fulfilling sexual life, so can unrealistic expectations. Many children are not only pressured into high-status jobs but are also pressured to be the absolute "best" at all times.

Even in the 1990s, over the objections of psychologists, children are still rejected by parents or demeaned by them if they do not come first in class or hit home runs or win every popularity contest. These parental admonitions are mentally absorbed by the child, later to become part of his conscience as an adult.

As a result, many men and women are tense, angry, and depressed on the job and off because they do not achieve at work the equivalent of an *A*+ or a home run every day. Just as it is important for parents and teachers to help children enjoy their school work, it is important for all of us to realize that to be successful on the job our prime concern should be the pleasure the work offers rather than exclusive dependence on the visible signs of success.

I recall working with Mary, thirty-eight, unmarried, who sold insurance. She was a successful salesperson, highly esteemed by her colleagues and superiors. But certain months she failed to sell a million dollars' worth of insurance and therefore could no longer be a member of the "million dollar club." Depressed and irritable, Mary would then gamble indiscriminately at the racetrack, as though to say to her bosses, "I don't give a damn about money."

I helped Mary understand that at these times of low self-esteem she was reliving in her work an aspect of her childhood. As a child, she had felt unloved by both parents unless she reached the top of her class and indeed became superior in anything she undertook.

Her mother and father never talked of the pleasure of working, and she never realized that she considered trivial rather than crucial the fun of relating to clients and the stimulation in arranging creative life-insurance polices.

As I helped Mary focus on the pleasures that could be derived from her work, rather than the sum that would be paid, not only did she feel better, like herself more, but she found that the money did follow. Like many of us, Mary had been deeply influenced by a questionable view of the work ethic. She felt that if work does not give pleasure but pain, then she was doing something worthwhile.

It is only in recent decades that industry, and the workplace in general, recognizes that productive work emerges when the worker is happy with his activities, peers, and supervisors. Recently the Swedish Parliament asked the question, "Should we try to promote feet that adapt to shoes or should we make shoes that fit the feet?" The Parliament was implying that rather than forcing people to adjust to a stressful work environment, employers should focus on changing the work itself. Sweden is carrying out an idea that is becoming more prevalent throughout the world: employers are learning to adapt work conditions to the physical and psychological conditions of people. In other words, the shoe should be fitted to the foot and employees given opportunities to take part in arranging their work situation, even transforming it.

To feel successful and to like ourselves, we have to enjoy our work. We also have to like those with whom we work. When we feel unhappy on the job we may be in the wrong job or the trouble may lie in the conditions of the job. But most often satisfaction on the job can be achieved if we are honest with ourselves.

This means we are doing what we really want to do, adapting to the conditions, changing what we can. We are also, most important, speaking frequently to the child within, who often is the greatest disrupter of working conditions. We listen to his demands, then if we feel they are not realistic, proceed with our own more mature evaluation of the benefits of the work in which we are engaged. This is part of truly growing up, recognizing that there is still part of us defying true maturity.

CHAPTER 6

SPORTS SLUMPS

In his book *Timebends* Arthur Miller, the famous playwright, talks about his brother Kermit. He asks:

> Why did Kermit nearly always fall just a step or two before the final line in the Central Park races we were constantly running? The crowd of boys from the row of apartment houses facing the park on 110th Street was cheering him on, his powerful legs were pumping along at a good steady pace, and just as he spread out his arms, down he went and lost. What choice of his lay behind this? Was it unrelated to his volunteering for the Army in World War II and as an Infantry Captain finding himself carrying a man on his back for hours in zero weather until they could reach an aid station, while his own toes were freezing and becoming gangrenous? Whence come these fateful images that might lose a man his feet, or his life—or

> be your salvation if he happens to be near when you need saving?

Miller does not answer his own questions about why his brother turned out to be a regular loser. But he offers many speculations, all the way from altruism to masochism. He even suggests that Kermit's defeatist life-style was related to the rest of his life, that Kermit emerged as a loser almost everywhere along the line:

> Once Kermit laid hands on a clock or a machine of any kind, it died, as though of fright, its leftover parts hidden under vases and inside the piano where suddenly he would rediscover them, after months had passed, and attack the ailing machine again.

While Miller suggests several possibilities as to why his brother was unable to stand on his own two feet except when he took care of those who were wounded, Arthur fails to talk about the most pertinent issue—that Kermit's brother, the outstanding, brilliant Arthur Miller, was extremely competent in almost anything he undertook and that next to him Kermit felt like a poorly coordinated, depressed loser and certainly not in his brother's league.

Sports of all types involve competition, and in many ways the participants compete for the love and admiration of the crowds, just as siblings compete for their parents' love. Whether it is tennis or boxing, where two rivals compete, or whether it is baseball, basketball, or any other team sport, rivalry between the contestants is paramount.

Inhibiting Aggression Can Be Harmful

If Kermit Miller were on a psychoanalyst's couch talking about the races he had lost in Central Park, he would probably reveal fantasies in which he was trying to defeat Arthur. But by everything we can determine from Arthur's biography, Arthur, as Kermit experienced him, was a warm and loving brother. Therefore it would be extremely difficult for Kermit to compete successfully with the outstanding brother he loved and who loved him.

Yet Kermit could stand on his own two feet when he ministered to somebody who did not take the place of Arthur, such as a wounded soldier. Here competition did not exist, sibling rivalry was not activated, and Kermit could succeed. We might speculate that if Kermit had entered a contest in the army to determine the best rescuer, he would have probably lost because the competitive, rivalrous situation would recur and Kermit would once again have to contend with unacceptable, competitive fantasies toward his brother.

If Kermit had written his own biography, he might have revealed some of his memories during the first three years of his life, prior to his brother's birth. We might have learned that up to the time Arthur was born, Kermit felt as most first-borns do, like His Majesty the King. Arthur's birth probably made King Kermit feel displaced from his throne as the bulk of parental attention turned to King Arthur. Dethroned Kermit would be furious and probably want to eliminate the new king.

But like most angry three-year-olds who want and need their parents' love, Kermit instead used his aggression to demean himself. By ministering to the wounded, Kermit could deny that he wanted to wound Arthur and other rivals. In many ways, Kermit probably felt like a "wounded soldier" himself, someone who was out of the running and therefore could look after those with whom he felt emotional kinship.

To understand losers in sports we have to know the dynamics of rivalry. Many athletes, professional and amateur, Little Leaguers and major leaguers, although able and skillful, talented and energetic, like Kermit, renounce victory and remain underdogs. Many an able athlete experiences the rivalry inherent in the athletic event as sibling rivalry and cannot tolerate defeating what in his fantasy appears as a brother or sister.

A college student of eighteen was referred to me for counseling by his wrestling coach. The coach was convinced that Don had ability and talent that he was not using. When I met Don, he spoke softly, seeming mild-mannered and inhibited when it came to talking about his feelings.

Slowly Don and I discovered through his dreams and fantasies that he felt very resentful toward his brother Rob, who was four years younger. Rob appeared to him to be his parents' favorite. Don told me his brother did not have to struggle, as he did, for love and approval, which came to Rob naturally. While Don was talking to me one day about his resentment toward his brother, he confessed, "I can't stand the no-good brat. I'd like to nail him down and forever."

"In other words you'd like to pin him on a wrestling mat and keep him there," I said.

Don soon realized that every time he entered into a wrestling match, unconsciously he wanted to kill his opponent, whom he fantasized as his brother. Then Don hated himself for his murderous rage.

Just as the person with academic and business failures

cannot tolerate fantasies full of rage, suppresses them, then punishes himself by failing courses or missing opportunities, many an athlete emerges as a loser because to win becomes in his mind the equivalent of destroying a brother or sister.

Sibling battles are not the only ones fought in the sports arena. An athlete may not be able to savor victory because in his mind he destroys a parent.

Floyd Patterson was the heavyweight champion of the world at twenty-one and the first boxer in his class to regain the title. He told of his feelings in an interview with Lucy Freeman, adapted from "A Twenty-Cent Bag of Candy," in *Celebrities on the Couch:*

Patterson began, "You can't say I've been on the couch. And I don't know exactly what you'd call the help I've received. But I know that I got on the right track because of the two years I spent at the Wiltwyck School for Boys. That's a place where they give help to boys in trouble. As a boy I was in trouble. I stole and played hooky from school. But I never did again after I left Wiltwyck because of what happened there.

"When I first arrived, I hated Wiltwyck, like any youngster would, sent away from home. I withdrew into a shell. But something happened after I had been there about two months. There was a teacher, Miss Vivian Costen, who tried to help me, and who seemed to like me very much. She made me feel I wasn't stupid. She told me, 'You don't have to be one hundred percent right. Everybody is wrong at times.' Then she handed me a twenty-cent bag of candy she was carrying. I took it. From then on, I was happy at Wiltwyck. I felt for the first time there was someone I could talk to.

"If I didn't understand something in class, Miss Costen would go over and over it with me. She would never get angry because I didn't catch on right away. Most of the time I had the right answer so I didn't feel stupid any more."

Inner Conflicts That Cause Anxiety

Many times an athlete turns his sports competition into a fantasied competition for a woman or, if the athlete is a woman, for a man. I once counseled a baseball pitcher who came to me because he realized he could pitch far better than he was doing. He had a vague feeling that his mounting losses stemmed from a strong psychological base but could not figure out his conflicts by himself.

Norm was twenty years old, a likeable, six-foot-tall youth, with obvious pitching talent who came to me for counseling. He described in detail his pitching forays: "When I warm up I feel terrific. I walk to the mound with confidence and enthusiasm. At the start of the game I get the ball over the plate and strike out many of the men. My curves and fast ball are hard for them to see and for about three innings it's terrific. Then something happens. I feel weak and tired. I can hardly throw the ball. It's as if I've lost my motivation, my confidence, my poise, and my energy."

Norm described the contrast between the way he warmed up, with confidence and energy, then pitched well for several innings, only to fall apart. After he described this scenario several times, he reminded me of a man who feels excited and stimulated while making love, then suddenly becomes impotent. His description of a pleasurable feeling while warming up was equivalent to the pleasure in sexual foreplay. His confidence and enthusiasm during the first few innings sounded like a man enjoying lovemaking and feeling potent until a limp, tired feeling took over, the way a man describes sexual impotency.

Because Norm's pitching scenario sounded so much like an unfulfilled sex life, I asked about his sexual experiences. At first he seemed to think I was a dirty old man or an unscientific Freudian when I tried to equate pitching a ball with a sexual thrust. But he was so eager to resolve his baseball slump that he was soon willing to describe his sexual life. Not surprisingly, his sexual experiences with women did appear to be quite similar to the way he functioned on the baseball field. He described his feelings when instigating foreplay as potent and enthusiastic during the initial stages. Then he would suffer premature ejaculations that left him dejected and the woman unfulfilled and unhappy.

When Norm could see the similarity between his sexual performance and his athletic performance, he could explore why he had to fail at both. What did we learn?

Norm and I discovered that he viewed his female sexual partners as objects that he enjoyed taking away from their male friends. To Norm, every woman was the property of another man, as his mother had been to his father, and he felt like a hostile thief stealing her body. This powerful fantasy was related to his early life.

His mother was seductive, he recalled, and he secretly competed with his father for her love. He tried to appear more masculine and more charming than his father, whom he wanted to "out-Casanova." Because he also loved and needed his father, Norm felt very guilty about his romantic and sexual fantasies toward his mother (and later with all other women). While Norm and I were discussing his angry, competitive attitudes toward sex, he made me the father figure who gave him permission to possess feelings natural to a little boy (though not to an emotionally mature adult man).

Slowly Norm started to feel less guilty. He allowed himself to be more potent, both in bed and on the pitching mound. Without realizing the symbolism in his statement, he said, toward the end of his counseling experience, "I don't need to be knocked out of the box any more. I can stay to the finish and not feel like a robber."

He thus told me that he had lost his guilt over the early sexual feelings toward his mother. He no longer had to take women from other men in order to have sex but now sought women uninvolved with other men.

I was delighted two years later to receive a letter saying he was still pitching and had met and married "a wonderful young woman" with whom he was preparing to raise children. Perhaps not fully realizing the meaning of his words, he wrote, "We're going to be a good team, play ball with each other and have a ball."

His last line read, "None of this would have been possible without the many months I worked with you. I felt healed in a new way that sure paid off."

Norm could now live a far fuller life, in part because I was an ardent baseball fan but primarily because I always enjoy helping men and women cope with childhood fantasies so that they may live more productively and pleasurably.

When men and women enter into competitive sports they inevitably bring with them all kinds of competitive battles from their life stories. Sometimes these battles spur them on to triumphs they savor. But they often feel guilty about their wishes to vanquish rivals.

Without realizing it, many a boxer unconsciously imagines he is in the ring waging war with a father or brother. But when he seeks to destroy a family member, he cannot carry out the act with equanimity. He feels himself to be an evil person who deserves punishment for wanting to hurt someone in his family. When an athlete, professional or amateur, does not play up to par, he often feels guilty about doing away with someone he loves or once loved.

Ruth, a twenty-year-old, attractive college student came to me for help. Although an extremely competent athlete, she would frequently lead her volleyball team to defeat. This was particularly true when the team seemed on the road to victory.

In one game Ruth's team was ahead 19–10 and needed only two points to win. Nearing victory, she found herself making poor serves and weak shots and as a result her team lost. She realized something was going on that kept her from letting her team win. During her sessions we sought to find out what that something was.

We discovered that, as the eldest daughter of three girls, Ruth often wished to rally her sisters into a team that would defy and devastate their parents. She never thought of acting on this fantasy, but when she played volleyball with other girls, she unconsciously turned her teammates into sisters, and a volleyball victory to her became the crushing of what she thought were sometimes mean and unlovable parents.

The idea of destroying her mother and father had become so overwhelming that frequently Ruth held back from winning. To lose in volleyball actually reassured her unconsciously that she was *not* a menacing daughter leading her sisters to a destructive attack on her parents. She suffered both ways now—whether she won or lost. If she won, in her mind she was a killer. If she lost, she was a weak sister in her fantasy. She was also a weak leader of her team.

It is very difficult for many athletes, as well as for many

sports fans, to realize that slumps and much of the choking up in various sports are expressions of acute anxiety. Anxiety always suggests there is some danger in the air.

When I have worked with athletes who cannot win despite possessing the talents and skills to do so, I try my best to help them get in touch with what they believe are the dangers in winning. As they talk to me of these dangers, they often feel their anxiety in the form of fast heartbeat, heavy breathing, or perhaps a headache. These are often the signs that their bodies are expressing the dangers in the air.

We then move to what the athletes are punishing themselves for and learn that, as with Ruth, they turn the athletic event into a destructive battle with their parents or, like Norm, mentioned earlier, into competition with other rivals from their pasts.

The True Victory

In any discussion of failure in sports we have to understand the meaning of victory. For many athletes, victory signifies that they are strong, competent people, to be admired. As long as they win, their self-esteem is bolstered. But if they lose, many feel they are incompetent, inadequate, and unlovable.

If we look at most losers after a game we can clearly see the deep depression in the players' faces, at times approaching utter despair, as if the world has come to an end. This was clearly evident when the Boston Red Sox baseball team lost to the New York Mets in 1986. After all the players had left the darkened Shea Stadium, Wade Boggs, the third baseman, sat alone on the bench and a photographer caught his profoundly sad expression as tears rolled down his cheeks.

Many a sports fan, after his team has lost an important or even an unimportant game, looks as if he is attending a funeral or is ready for his own. Victory and defeat, for those of us who live vicariously in the world of sports, become deeply distorted in our minds. We do not act as if we realize that it is quite possible to lose a sports event and still be a competent, lovable person. And when the fans boo a loser and the coach castigates the player not performing up to par, he is likely to feel publicly humiliated—as if he should be immediately fired from the team.

We have often seen, for example, the football player who misses a kick for the extra point act as if he has committed the most dastardly crime of the century. If we observe the reactions of the fans, we see they serve as the player's conscience and his woebegone face reveals that he is sure he deserves to be ostracized from the sport for years, if not for a lifetime.

For many athletes, women as well as men, victory conveys a macho image, one of strength and fortitude. Unfortunately, many athletes feel it essential to possess and keep this image. To lose means to them that they are wimps, comparable to men who cannot sexually perform.

Particularly in our competitive culture, where beating out the other person is admired and the importance of cooperation often overlooked, it should not surprise us that our attitude toward sports mirrors what takes place in society as a whole.

A man or woman who has not made a ton of money is frequently referred to contemptuously as a loser. An excellent movie or book is referred to as a winner. In our culture we idolize winners, believe they are to be admired, have everything going for them. We deplore and abhor losers, finding nothing admirable in them.

If we give just a glance to Little League baseball games we see young children, in some cases no older than eight, pressured by parents and coaches to perform like all-star major league players—at once. The children are severely criticized if they drop a ball or strike out. They feel humiliated and begin to hate themselves unless they hit a home run or catch every ball, even throws that go wild.

This pressure is unrelenting, and by the time the Little Leaguer reaches high school the intense pressure to be the constant victor runs very deep. It is a familiar sight at high school athletic events to see a coach raging and a young athlete gritting his teeth, trying to stop himself from throwing a temper tantrum or crying because he has, for the moment, failed to score.

The neurotic investment in athletic victories becomes even more apparent in college, where young men and women are given thousands of dollars in athletic scholarships for playing on the varsity team, even in some cases when they are close to illiterate. Although colleges and universities exist primarily for the purpose of educating young people in the arts and sciences, the status of athletes is often measured exclusively by their victories in athletic events.

Thus, many colleges and universities view sports not as an important dimension of the educational process, to give pleasure to the team members and the fans, but as a be-all and end-all, far more vital to the colleges and universities than anything else in the curriculum.

An example of how sports victories are overrated and overdramatized is the reaction of many alumni of Columbia University in New York City. Always regarded as a top-notch university when it comes to providing a top-notch education to top-notch young men and women, Columbia University for a number of years has had a football team that has lost most of its games. Regardless of the whys and wherefores of these losses, it is unfortunate that many alumni of the University have withdrawn financial and psychological support. In effect, these alumni are saying, "By their football victories ye shall judge them."

When we consider professional sports we are, of course, aware of the importance of victory, for professional athletes make a living by winning. It is important to recognize, however, that intense, hateful emotions frequently emerge in cutthroat competition.

The hatred in professional sports is usually quite feverish. Think of the many times during a baseball season that the players maul each other, as one side attacks the other because a pitcher has hit a batter with a pitched ball. Or the many soccer games in the past few years where not only did the players fight with each other, at times drawing blood, but fans killed each other, as happened in Europe a few years ago.

In tennis it is becoming a frequent event for a player to scream at a linesman or stare at him with hatred. This can ignite hatred in the fans.

The pleasure in destroying others and the cutthroat competition that pervades professional sports in particular, including ice hockey, basketball, and football, is rarely faced or discussed. Perhaps the cutthroat competition and hatred that can lead to death in some sports has been with us ever since the days of primitive man. However, very few anthropologists or other social scientists have attempted to understand the unleashing of such deep hatred in athletic events. We need to learn more about it.

A Pitcher's Brave Venture into Therapy

Jim Bouton in the late 1960s wrote *Ball Four,* a book that described in detail the politics in baseball, the feverish competition that induces deep anger, the ostracism of players who want to respect and love rather than to hate, and the alcoholism and other immature and inappropriate behavior so prevalent among baseball players.

Bouton, an outstanding pitcher for the New York Yankees, was isolated from baseball's mainstream because, like the honest doctor in Ibsen's *Enemy of the People,* he told the truth about dishonest and unprofessional practices.

Major league owners and other baseball personnel cannot tolerate seeing in print accounts of the unfair business practices that exist at times in baseball, the cruelty, even at times the sadism, of managers and coaches, as well as the unkind attitudes of players toward each other. This applies also to the obvious biases of some umpires who, as can be attested to by those who watch the games on television, sometimes make very unfair decisions. It is difficult to know with certainty if they are deliberate or unintended.

James Patrick Brosnan gave this account of his experiences, adapted from "The Reluctant Hero" in *Celebrities on the Couch:* "How did I happen to go into psychoanalysis? Because Art Meyerhoff told me to do it. Art, who later became one of my close friends, was head of his own advertising agency in Chicago and a stockholder in the Chicago Cubs. When I met him, I was eighteen and had been playing in the Cubs' minor league system. It was my first year in organized baseball, what was to be the first of nine lonely years in the minor leagues.

"I found out later that the Cubs' general manager, Jim Gallagher, had gone to Art, knowing he was interested in psychoanalysis as well as in the Cubs, and said, 'We've got a boy who has great talent but he's also got problems. What do you suggest?' Meyerhoff said, 'Bring him to me.' He suggested when I visited him in his office that I see a psychoanalyst, Dr. George Mohr. I decided I would try it and called up Dr. Mohr, a well-known Chicago psychoanalyst, made an appointment to visit him. I got the impression from Dr. Mohr that he thought continued sessions would be of some help, so I went twice a week at first, then three times a week. He did not know much about baseball but that was all right with me. I preferred not to talk about baseball outside the ball park."

Jim could not have sessions during the baseball year, when he had to travel all over the country, but when the season ended in October, not to be resumed until March, Jim returned to Dr. Mohr's office on Michigan Avenue faithfully for several years. He wrote, "I went three times a week. I did not lie on the couch very often but sat tete-à-tete with Dr. Mohr. It seemed easier to talk that way, and I was beginning to face some of my problems.

"I found that now I could discuss myself more freely, especially my feelings about my father. I was the oldest of six children and he and I always had a strained relationship. I started to understand that this was the basis for my rebellion against managers, umpires, or any sort of authority.

"I always had trouble with umpires. (I see how clearly this is related to my father, who was an umpire for a while.) Once Jocko Conlan, a National League umpire, said to me, 'I want to talk to you. Your reputation is bad among umpires.'

" 'Why?' I asked.

" 'Your attitude is bad,' he said. 'Why don't you change

it? You'll be a better pitcher and get along better with everyone.'

"If an umpire or manager made a decision I thought unfair, I would blow my stack. This was something I realized I would have to overcome. I believe I've done so. Some of my best friends today are umpires."

Jim also wrote, "It was difficult for me to realize that it was not just one parent who contributed to my lack of cooperation with authorities, but both. I didn't like that at all. You have to have one parent to lean on, and if you feel both are, in a sense, your enemies, you are lost. Dr. Mohr and I discussed my relationship with my mother at quite some length.

"My mother, Rose, a former nurse, was an extremely intelligent woman. She loved music and reading, in contrast to my father, whose only interest was baseball. In time I combined both their interests, becoming both a professional baseball player and a writer. I recalled that when I was six or seven years old, I would go to the library every week and pick out books for my mother to read to me. My father would say, 'Don't read that junk—read this,' and hand me a rule book on baseball. I carried out my father's wishes by playing baseball and football as a boy. In high school, I grew to six feet one inch, but only weighed 114 pounds so that I looked like a stringbean."

As a result of Dr. Mohr's help, Jim said, "I was able to marry and have my own children. I had never thought of forming any enduring, intimate relationship with a woman. One night at a party I met a very attractive young woman named Anne Stewart Pitcher. I discovered we had at least two things in common, baseball and music. We were married six months later on June 23, 1952."

Jim finally was part of a pennant-winning team in 1961 when he pitched for the Cincinnati Reds in the World

Series. His first book, *The Long Season*, sold over twenty thousand copies. James Thurber wrote, "When it comes to writing, Brosnan has a good fast ball and a dazzling curve."

But at times Jim still felt depressed "in spite of all my good luck," and wanted to return to Dr. Mohr for further help, only to discover he had left Chicago. Jim consulted a woman analyst there, Dr. Lucia Tower, seeing her during the off-season of 1961 for three months, twice a week. He wrote, "She helped me through my depression, encouraged me to write my second book and to try fiction and poetry which I had long wanted to do, as well as write about subjects other than sports."

He summed up, "The help given me, first by Dr. Mohr and then by Dr. Tower, has, I feel, allowed me to communicate first, with myself, second, with Anne, and finally with other people." He added, "Without the help I received in the analysts' offices, I don't think I could have done this. In looking back, I feel that my analysis, my marriage, and knowing Art Meyerhoff were the most important steps I took toward a fuller, more satisfying life. I have reached an understanding of myself and know now that people are good to know for what they are, and not for what I am to them or can get out of them."

Jim showed that by understanding the buried conflicts in his mind he became a more loving human being and a more creative person. This enhanced his ability to cope as a ball player. He also said that his success in writing emerged from his experience in psychotherapy as "writing became an experience almost as rewarding as playing baseball."

There is today a profession called sports psychology in which psychologists study such factors as motivation, morale, the learning of skills, particularly those issues that interfere with individual and team performances. Sports psychologists work with players who have become drug addicts, alcoholics, or gamblers. They all agree that what transpires in a player's life off the sports field is more crucial than anything else in understanding his slumps on the field.

They have been able to show that if a player is going through a divorce, he may sink into a slump, or if he has conflicts with his parents or others that have remained unresolved, the same kind of failure on the field may ensue. Psychologists are now convinced that the mental health of the player is an important ingredient in success in sports. Many teams, including the New York Mets, have a psychological expert on their staff who advises both players and coaches.

At times the competition in sports is so intense that members hate each other and cannot cooperate to produce a winning team. To win, a team obviously needs cooperative teamwork. Yet many players who vie with each other for personal stardom forget they are a part of a team.

When we understand that an aggressive, destructive drive permeates many sports, it becomes clear why there are sports slumps, why so many athletes choke up so often. Nobody wants to kill without feeling some reservations about this dastardly deed. Particularly when the thought occurs as the athlete unconsciously turns his opponent into a family member, the wish for victory becomes very ambivalent.

I have worked with many athletes, amateur and professional, and have frequently heard the comment, "I want to win and badly, but I feel pretty horrible wanting to knock out a brother."

The unconscious object of such wrath may also be a mother, a father, or a sister. Our deepest rages arise when we are very young and have become extremely jealous of anyone who, we believe, takes away the love of a parent, or when we become angry at the parent for depriving us of love in one way or another.

Two of the major factors in sports slumps, only recently under consideration, are the importance of the human relationship between coach and team members and the relation of team members toward each other.

In team sports, cooperation among the players is absolutely necessary. For such cooperation to take place there must be mutual affection between manager and team. A parent who loves his children fosters warm feelings among the siblings. The same relationship occurs or fails to occur in sports. Many a slump by a player, many a series of losses by a team, can be attributed to undischarged anger that the team members have held back toward manager or coach.

The manager or coach of a team is likely to become a parental figure. If he is understanding, fair, and loving, his chances of directing a winning team are very much increased. But if he favors certain players or uses one or more as scapegoats, he will contribute toward team losses. When a coach speaks in derogatory fashion to a player in front of teammates, the team will gradually become demoralized and lose all chance of winning a pennant race.

In the 1990 baseball season Bud Harrelson, an excellent manager and coach, was leading the Mets into first place after they were practically in the cellar. His warmth, concern, and benign, fatherly attitude turned disaster into success. But Harrelson one day lost his cool. In the locker room, in front of all the players, he expressed contempt for a new first baseman, Mike Marshall, bought from the Los Angeles Dodgers. Mike had been complaining that he did not play enough. It was after Harrelson's tirade that the team started to lose once again. Team players identify with each other and even if they may dislike the player who is demeaned, they still resent the coach or manager for demeaning him. They reason, "If it happens to the other guy, it can happen to me."

When a coach or manager is understanding and thoughtful, the players' competitive spirit toward each other diminishes, and they cooperate to defeat a common opponent. It is insufficiently recognized in sports that a team failure is often an expression of rebellion against the coach or manager, much like a student who is resentful toward a hypercritical teacher and refuses to learn the subject assigned.

A tennis player on an outstanding college team once confessed to me, "In many ways I want my opponent to win because that's the only way I can spite my coach, whom I don't like." This attitude exists at all levels—in the Little League, in high school, college, and professional sports.

Sports slumps and team failures can usually be resolved if the player or players come to grips with something difficult to face—their wish to lose. If the athlete turns his opponent into a family member he wishes to vanquish, he will have to suppress those moves that insure victory because he is convinced he will then be a killer and that thought he cannot tolerate.

Sports slumps and team losses can be diminished if those involved do not view loss as death and victory as life. When they can like themselves even though they lose, there will be many fewer athletic failures at all levels of all sports.

The athlete, to be successful, has to control his hatred toward coaches, managers and other players. Often this requires discussion among the important actors in the sports drama. A good coach is like a good parent—loving, firm, and fair. A successful athlete must feel loved and supported and must be convinced that to win is not to kill and to lose is not to die.

CHAPTER 7

FAILURES IN EVERYDAY LIFE

A major finding of modern psychology is that virtually no act of human behavior happens by chance. Whom we choose or reject in love, what kind of work we perform, the interests or aversions we possess, where we go and what we do on vacation, what we seek and what we avoid, all are governed by a constellation of unconscious wishes, inner prohibitions, and emotionally charged memories.

As we have pointed out several times, in every human being there is a child who is busy loving, hating, and yearning. This child influences our adult behavior in a profound way. How cooperative or spiteful we are, how inhibited or free, how happy or sad, are all influenced by the child within us. Just as failures in love, work, sports, and school are in many ways arranged by the child within, so too are the more subtle failures that confront every one of us.

What Accidents Tell Us

Failures in everyday life include accidents in which we may physically hurt others or be hurt, lose important possessions, break valuables, or stumble and fall at inappropriate times. These accidents do not merely happen. Just as we unwittingly arrange for the kinds of failures we have discussed in previous chapters, such as failures in business, marriage, and parent-child relationships, we also arrange—although unconsciously—to forget names and appointments, make embarrassing slips of the tongue, and phrase provocative remarks which we insist we do not really mean.

You may ask, "Does a person truly arrange to slip on the ice?" Or "Is this individual causing a car accident?" Or "If someone stumbles and falls in the apartment, has he planned to do so?" Or "If I trip and find myself on the sidewalk and if there was a serious obstruction in the way, is it still all my fault?"

No, of course not. It is quite possible for accidents to befall us which we have not influenced at all or have influenced very little. We will discuss the phenomenon of persistent accidents and persistent errors in judgment leading to persistent failures of everyday life.

Modern psychology has also suggested that behavior, as we observe it, tells us little about the motives of the person who enacts that particular behavior. The only way we can be sure of the actual motives of everyday failures is to interview the person in depth. All of the human examples to which we now refer emanate from the productions of patients in psychotherapy or from men and women who have been carefully interviewed.

We do not have to be psychologists to know that when a man or woman is involved in more than one or two car accidents, eventually he or she has to take some responsibility for these mishaps. I recall a patient, Mary, a woman in her early thirties, who drove down from Stamford, Connecticut, to New York City for a session with me three times a week. After she told me of her third car accident on the highway within two months I began to investigate with her the nature of her feelings and thoughts when she was behind the wheel. Without much prodding on my part, Mary told me that while driving she would derive much pleasure from speeding on the highway and passing other drivers. As she whizzed by them she found herself feeling contempt, calling them dopes, jerks, and idiots.

For Mary, driving a car became like driving a tank on a field of battle. She wanted to pound away at everyone on the road. But like most people who are full of rage, Mary not only hated the other passengers but was convinced that they hated her.

Who did these drivers represent in Mary's past? Slowly she was able to realize that every time she stepped into her car she turned all other drivers into her brother, whom she openly despised. The other drivers also represented, but to a lesser extent, her mother, who she felt was never very emotionally responsive toward her and toward whom she bore some resentment over the years.

Like almost all persons filled with intense anger toward family members, Mary believed that she deserved punishment for her sadistic feelings. Consequently, every time she rammed into the rear of a car the front of her own car became as damaged as the rear of the car she hit.

Mary's car accidents are not atypical. Thousands of men, women, and young people who have persistent car accidents are unconsciously reenacting power struggles with family members and with others. They lash out at strangers, then feel guilty about their sadism, and, without realizing it, seek punishment for daring to express their rage.

Mary did not realize that she was seeking punishment for ploughing into another car until she almost lost her license. Sometimes a person does not realize how self-destructive he is until he ends up in a hospital with serious injuries or causes others to be injured.

An unplanned pregnancy is at times referred to as an accident. Frequently the woman, married or unmarried, who experiences these accidents believes that the pregnancy occurred by chance and not by design. I have been so interested in this phenomenon that I conducted two extensive research projects on the subject. One was on men responsible for pregnancies that were consciously not wanted and the other on pregnant women, largely unmarried, who did not intend to become pregnant.

The study that I directed on men involved in unwanted pregnancies was conducted in the United States Army during the Korean War while I was an officer in a mental health consultation center at Fort Dix, New Jersey. Inasmuch as my work involved counseling soldiers who were in all kinds of trouble, I met several who sought my help because they had "knocked up" one or more young women.

As I interviewed dozens of these men I learned that in over 90 percent of the cases of unwanted pregnancy, no form of contraception was used. When I asked the subjects about this, I found that only in rare cases were contraceptives not used because of religious convictions. Most of the men could have prevented impregnating the woman if they had really wished to do so.

I learned that for most of these young men the pregnancy became a hidden, though at times not so hidden, indication of their virility. After revealing visible signs of distress during an interview, often they would smile on recalling that indeed they had impregnated the woman. Several bragged of this, talked proudly about their sexual potency, or the number of sperm cells within them. I discovered that the majority of these men viewed sex as some kind of athletic triumph inasmuch as the term *scored* was frequently used.

In addition to trying to reassure themselves of their masculinity, many of my subjects by impregnating a woman unwittingly revealed some of their desperation in leaving home and families. Several, on reflection, realized that the pregnancy was a way of trying to avoid the possibility of their girlfriend's separating from them. At this time, the early 1950s, abortion was rarely considered a legitimate alternative. Consequently, when the young woman became pregnant a forced marriage often ensued, solidifying the relationship, at least symbolically.

During a war sexual relations often occur because of the imminent threat of death, not because love is an essential part of the sexual act.

In my research in the 1960s on what was then referred to as the unmarried mother, I learned a great deal about the family background of such women. In almost every case there was a problematic relationship between the young woman and her father. In most cases, the father was experienced as a man who, on occasion, could be warm and stimulating but often emotionally and physically unavailable. In other words, many of these young women felt stimulated by their fathers on the one hand but abandoned on the other.

What does a young woman feel when she is loved, then rejected? Stimulated, then abandoned? She begins to doubt that she is lovable and feminine. She questions whether she did something to provoke her father's withdrawal. Often these women had mothers who were not loved and admired by their husbands, who sought other women. This compounded the daughter's negative view of her own femininity. "If you love my mother, you love me; if you hate my mother and leave her for another woman, you hate me," the daughter often reasons.

To become pregnant was one way for these confused young women to prove to themselves that they were loved, at least for the moment. Often the man with whom a young woman engaged in sexual relations was a friend of long duration but who shared a characteristic of the woman's father—a man who could not be trusted for too long and would probably leave her, as her father did.

Some of these women felt such acute resentment toward their fathers that the pregnancy was something they did not wish to share with the biological father. They abandoned the man in the same fashion they felt abandoned; he was no longer a part of their life. It was as if they denied he had any participation in the pregnancy. They said, in effect, "Scram!" They felt this was what they were told to do by their father.

Losses That Reveal Our Rage

Other kinds of accidents are not as self-destructive as car accidents or unwanted pregnancies but tell of discomfort and anxiety in the person who arranges them.

Consider the phenomenon of losing possessions such as wallets, jewelry, glasses, briefcases, gloves, and other valued items that may not be essential to life but are considered very important in making existence more pleasurable.

One way a psychologist tries to understand why somebody might lose a possession is to ask himself, "Why would this person unconsciously *want* to lose this particular item?" Usually if a person tries to answer this question he can find some of the reasons for his losses.

A patient of mine lost his wallet on three different occasions. Consciously, Ben, a man in his forties, became extremely upset and castigated himself whenever his wallet disappeared. After this happened a third time, I tried to help him explore the thoughts and feelings that may have been buried within him and that precipitated the losses.

While at first Ben could think of nothing, slowly he began to perceive certain connections. It turned out that the three times he lost his wallet there were several fairly large checks in it and each time one of the checks in the lost wallet was made out to me.

It did not take us long to realize that Ben did not want to pay me, inasmuch as he was feeling some latent resentment toward me as psychotherapist. Rather than consciously express this resentment for what he later referred to as paid friendship, he was making sure, although unconsciously, that I would not get paid.

Two of the other checks that Ben lost were for an attorney and a physician—helping professionals with whom Ben also wanted a free ride. Unconsciously he wished that his physician, his attorney, and his psychotherapist were loving parents who nurtured him because they loved him, not specialists who wanted to help him in order to make a living. As Ben could express his resentment toward me and toward other helpers in his life, past and present, he no longer lost his wallet and the checks in it.

A young woman, Margaret, age thirty, also a patient, lost her wallet frequently. But her reasons for doing so were very different from Ben's. As Margaret and I tried to learn what was going on in her unconscious to cause her to lose her wallet, we discovered she usually lost it while on a date with a young man. She would leave her wallet in ladies' rooms or at the table in restaurants. The loss of her wallet usually induced in her date deep sympathy, support, and concerned activity. The man would make phone calls and inquiries in an effort to find the lost wallet.

Margaret and I discovered that she loved the attention of the men who "took care of me." She had experienced both of her parents as rather cold and detached. By unconsciously arranging for her date to be concerned about her loss, she was guaranteeing that she would receive some much-desired mothering and fathering.

Losing wallets and other possessions have different meanings for different individuals. For Ben, it was an act of defiance; for Margaret, it was a disguised cry for nurturing. For someone else, it could be a strong unconscious wish for punishment or humiliation.

I have seen many men and women who felt guilty about making money later arrange to feel like a thief. Not only did they lose checks or cash but in several cases they tore up a check they received in the mail, consciously thinking it was an advertisement. A patient of mine had been taught in a rigid way that it is better to give than to receive. Wherever he went, beforehand he bought a gift. But then he would frequently misplace or lose the present. Without realizing it, he resented bestowing it on another person.

Often we throw away by mistake something valuable to express an anger we do not fully recognize. One patient twice threw away his birth certificate. He confessed to me that he was embarrassed and ashamed to have been born in Russia. Rather than acknowledge his true feelings about his birthplace he confiscated the birth certificate and discarded it.

We feel much consternation and embarrassment when we break articles around the house such as cups, drinking glasses, eye glasses, or precious antiques. Often when we destroy something "by accident," we are expressing feelings that are quite difficult to confront.

One woman broke a valuable antique glass tray at a friend's party, "purely by accident," she claimed. When she realized she had not even apologized, she became curious about her motives. On later reflection she discovered she was jealous of the hostess because her husband had been quite openly amorous toward the attractive hostess. Rather than admit her jealousy and fury she "accidentally on purpose" broke the hostess's valuable tray.

A doctoral student, Jill, who was constantly breaking or losing her eyeglasses, began to examine this habitual and expensive act. She said to me one day, "I want to know what is going on in my unconscious that causes me to do this." Several days later she confided, "Professor, you'll be proud of me. I figured out why I'm always breaking and losing my eyeglasses. If I don't have my glasses, I can't work on my dissertation. So you and I better talk about why I'm so reluctant to complete my doctoral studies."

For Jill to complete her doctoral studies meant to her that she would have to be an independent woman, no longer supported like a little girl by doting parental figures called professors, who represented the doting parents of her infancy.

Seemingly accidental acts such as breaking eyeglasses can obscure difficulties we do not wish to face. Jill lost her glasses to hide the fact that she felt very uncomfortable about assuming the role of a mature woman. Ben, in the earlier example, arranged to lose his wallet rather than face his resentment at paying money to professionals for helping him. This also masked a deeper fear—the fear of maturing, which meant giving up the illusions and fears of childhood.

Just as Kermit Miller, Arthur Miller's brother, could not complete most tasks because he was too frightened to surpass his more competent, better-known younger brother, many of us lose and break objects because we do not want to face hidden rivalries, hidden resentments, and hidden fears of punishment.

In the everyday life of the army I frequently observed one soldier dropping on another a tray heaped high with food. I learned that in most cases the other soldier was a superior officer or a sergeant toward whom the one who dropped the tray felt resentment for one reason or another.

We can usually find hidden resentments within ourselves when we step on someone's toe, bump into him, spill something on him, or break one of his cherished possessions. This is our unconscious form of attack on someone we feel has hurt us.

Why We Sometimes "Forget"

A very common, perhaps universal failure in everyday life not well understood is that of forgetting. All of us forget at times. We cannot remember the names of people, chores we have to perform, appointments we have made, telephone calls we did not answer.

Usually when we forget to do something we concoct rationalizations to excuse ourselves. We feel under great pressure, we face many priorities to fulfill, we are too tired, aching, or ill to accomplish normal tasks.

Few of us, even the most sophisticated, are willing to accept the psychological truth that in most instances we forget because we *want* to forget and we remember because we *want* to remember. While it is also true that as we get older and as less blood flows to the brain, our weaker-functioning circulatory system does lessen our ability to remember. But it is still true that whether we are twenty-five or ninety-five years old, we tend to remember what we wish to remember and to forget what we wish to forget.

Many people, particularly senior citizens, fail to recall what day of the week it is but do remember something that transpired sixty-five years ago—not only the day of the week but the exact hour the event occurred.

I worked in psychotherapy with a man in his eighties who had come to see me because he felt deeply depressed and was afraid of dying. He would frequently forget the day or the time of our appointment. Yet he would always remember the time and day he was going to attend such events as baseball games, weddings, reunions, and other occasions that afforded him much pleasure.

My patient, Sidney, like most senior citizens, wanted to attribute his forgetfulness to Alzheimer's disease, brain damage, senility, and other organic causes. While I felt it was conceivable his hypotheses might have some validity, I nonetheless tried to help him realize there might be some nonorganic reasons that could contribute to his forgetfulness.

One day I asked him, "Can you think of any of the reasons why you want to remember the date and time of a baseball game that occurred over fifty years ago but cannot recall our weekly appointment on Tuesdays at ten o'clock?"

After several protests, in which Sidney attributed his forgetfulness to everything from senile dementia to insomnia, he finally began to reflect seriously on my questions. He said, with some embarrassment, "I guess I like baseball better than psychotherapy and I also like looking at the pitcher Tom Seaver more than I like looking at you, particularly when you make me talk about my problems."

Without realizing it, Sidney was explaining why most of us forget what we wish to forget and remember what we wish to remember. Numerous psychological experiments have demonstrated over and over again that we have a great propensity to recall what we have enjoyed and are strongly inclined to forget events or issues that stir up our anxieties and our conflicts.

If we wish to improve our memory one of the best ways to do it is to let our minds try to explore our feelings toward the person or place, appointment or date, that we cannot remember. As we permit ourselves to daydream, we will start to feel some uncomfortable emotions. If these emotions are not suppressed but accepted as belonging to us, in all probability we will eventually recall in detail what we have forgotten.

When Sidney was helped to feel the understandable and very human resentment and embarrassment of sitting in the office of a psychoanalyst and when he felt safe enough to discuss this with me, he began to remember the day and exact time of his weekly appointments. Instead of acting out his resentment by forgetting his appointments, he could talk about the real issues—his embarrassment, fears, and resentments. His memory started to improve almost at once.

Many people assume that if their memory constantly fails them, they suffer from limited intelligence. If Alzheimer's and other organic diseases are not assigned the cause, people with poor memories call themselves stupid. If those with uncertain memories were truly stupid, we would not have so many absentminded professors!

The absentminded professor can tell you the date, the author, and the publisher of an obscure book, but he does not know where he left his shoes and sometimes cannot remember for hours. Or he can give you verbatim some highly technical material from a book on philosophy or physics that he read ten years ago, but he has no memory whatsoever of where he put his keys yesterday. He can without hesitating for a second call up the names of foreign authors but can't remember the names of his current students.

Does all this happen because the professor is stupid? Definitely not. What some professors remember gives them great pleasure and stimulation and what they forget are the irritants in their lives. They are much more devoted and dedicated to authors and books written fifty years ago than they are to their students, their keys, or their shoes.

Many an absentminded professor has told me without embarrassment, "I could get my work done if I didn't have to meet with the students in class." Though their students, in theory, should be their number one priority, some professors prefer to forget them and concentrate on their research. Although they need shoes to walk to class, since they do not want to go to class they cannot find their shoes. Many an absentminded professor loses all kinds of personal articles but interestingly, if he is an avid reader and does not feel guilty about his appetite in this area, he rarely loses his books or journals.

It is much easier to understand why we might forget an appointment with a doctor or a dentist. They can physically hurt us, and to avoid the pain they may inflict we forget about our appointments with them and spare ourselves the pain. Forgetting is much easier than postponing because when we forget we put the appointment with the dentist or doctor out of our minds but when we postpone we hang on to our obligation and have to cope with the anticipated pain.

How do we account for the forgetting of certain names that seem innocuous, neutral, nothing to be ashamed of? The fact is that when we forget a name, we are not feeling neutral but are warding off emotions that stir some discomfort or shame.

I worked with a young unmarried couple who were seriously considering marriage. They had mixed feelings about taking the vows and wanted premarital counseling to see if they could resolve their mixed feelings.

Bob and Shirley were in their early thirties. While they were fond of each other, both suffered from strong inhibitions regarding emotional closeness and intimacy. This was the issue we worked on in their counseling.

One day, as Bob and Shirley acknowledged that they now felt closer and more relaxed in each other's company, they described their excitement for one another while attending a New York Mets baseball game. As they did so, both blocked from memory the name of the home-team pitcher who had won it. They had watched him pitch many times and over the years had often read about him in the newspapers, yet they could not recall his name.

They left the session frustrated. But the following week they entered the consultation room wearing broad smiles. Bob said to me, even before they sat down, "You know what the name of the player is?"

Shirley announced, "Ron Darling!"

It was not too difficult for Bob and Shirley to realize they both felt closer to each other and were thinking seriously of marrying but still felt anxious and worried about setting a date. Each wanted to call the other "darling" but felt too uncomfortable to use the word. The forgetting was a mutual attempt, an unconscious one, to gain some distance from one another because they were still frightened of marrying.

Every time we forget a date or a name such as "Darling," we should ask ourselves what feelings or thoughts we are trying to repress. Like Sidney, like Bob and Shirley, all of us forget in order to protect ourselves from something we believe may bring discomfort.

Most of the memories that we do not wish to recall are not remembered because to think of them would activate pain. We want to forget about a friend who hurt us, a relative who shunned us, a boss who fired us. However, we often do recall events, people, and places that induced pain and embarrassment: We remember what we think we would like to forget, and we forget what we think we would like to remember. The explanation for this seeming paradox lies in the fact that we are unconsciously looking for punishment. If we conjure up painful memories again and again, we can tell ourselves that we feel like guilty children who need to suffer in order to punish ourselves.

Whenever we keep recalling the repugnant and the distasteful, we should ask, "What am I punishing myself for?" and try to be honest with ourselves about the issue or issues causing us to feel so guilty.

Mitchell, a man in his forties, came for help because he felt very depressed. His marriage of twelve years was collapsing, he enjoyed only limited pleasure in living and felt miserable most of the hours he was awake.

He recalled one memory that haunted him. When he was eight years old he wet his pants one day in school and suffered a deep humiliation, though none of his classmates became aware of his accident because he waited for everyone to leave the room before he stood up. Mitchell was constantly upset by this event that only he knew about. Three decades later in my office he experienced it as though it had happened the day before.

This sort of self-flagellation occurs in all of us but few

know why. We dig up memories of acts suffered thirty or more years ago as though they had just taken place, because we are currently feeling deep shame and guilt. Although it took Mitchell many sessions to face why he obsessed about wetting his pants at the age of eight, we finally came up with the answer.

He could eventually say, "I'm pissed off in the present, particularly at work, I'm obviously not happy with my wife who wants to leave me, and I'd like to vent all my anger at everyone in the office and my wife. But if I dare discharge a sign of rage, I'll feel like the silly, stupid boy who wet his pants years ago, and expect everyone to laugh at me."

He was quiet a moment, then went on, "Just as I was angry at the teacher and my parents for all the pressures they placed on me and would have liked to piss all over them, this is how I now feel toward my wife, bosses and colleagues. I still feel as I did at eight."

Because Mitchell could feel safe in discharging his resentments about both the present and past, realizing I did not disapprove of him as he did so, the ugly early memory receded. He no longer felt the need to castigate himself for he could accept with more equanimity his rage in the present that was reminiscent of his rage of the past. Like Mitchell, many of us obsess about past humiliations to punish ourselves for current resentments.

What Slips of the Tongue Reveal

Another universal failure of everyday life is the slip of the tongue, sometimes referred to as a Freudian slip. It applies to those times we say what we consciously do not want to reveal.

I will never forget an experience from my first year in private practice of psychotherapy when a man called me on the telephone. He wanted to say, "I'm desperately in need of help," but what emerged was "I'm desperately in need of trouble."

When John, age forty-five, arrived at my office, he seemed dejected and depressed. He told me, "I think it's only my fantasy but I can't help feeling that my wife is having an affair with a man who is much handsomer, far more brilliant, and richer than I am."

These proved to be mere fantasies. His wife was a dedicated, devoted woman who loved him deeply. Somehow John was desperately in need of "trouble," the word that slipped out when he meant to say "help."

He did not feel entitled to a loving wife. He had fantasies of wishing to cheat on her and projected them onto her, as though she were the culprit and he had to suffer from her infidelity. In other words, he unconsciously wished to seek danger and trouble. Like many people, he felt uncomfortable with a loving spouse, wanted to find out what other women were like.

Our slips of the tongue tell us the truth. I recall the many times I was introduced before speeches where for one reason or another the person introducing me had mixed feelings toward me. Once a colleague who disagreed with many of my psychological beliefs wanted to say, "I now present Dr. Strean." Instead he said, "I now prevent Dr. Strean."

Another time the gentleman chosen to introduce me arrived late. He intended to say, "It is with pleasure that I introduce Dr. Strean." Instead he said, "It is with pressure I introduce Dr. Strean."

A third time when I was on tour to promote a book, a woman introduced me to three different audiences. She must have started to resent this because during the second introduction, when she meant to say "Dr. Strean makes difficult ideas sound easy," she said, "Dr. Strean makes easy ideas sound difficult." On the third introduction her latent resentment emerged quite clearly as she told the audience, "To miss hearing Dr. Strean speak is the chance of a lifetime."

All these slips of the tongue aroused laughter. We laugh when we hear them because we feel relieved that the real truth has emerged and the tension from holding back the truth has disappeared. The persons who "slipped" when they introduced me revealed their genuine resentment toward me and my ideas. But they could not be aware of this consciously and thus the slip of the tongue revealed the truth.

Perhaps the most unforgettable slip of the tongue that I witnessed occurred on television. Just prior to going on the air, the interviewer had made it plain that he disagreed with all I had written in my book *Resolving Marital Conflicts.* When we finally went on camera, he was prepared to introduce me as "a distinguished professor from Rutgers University." Instead he announced, "Dr. Strean is a disgusting professor from Rutgers University."

Slips of the tongue (and the mind) are shown when we kiss or hug the wrong person at a party, show up at the wrong place at the wrong time, oversleep, overeat, or overspend. These slips tell us the truth about ourselves. Whether the slip appears as an innocuous mistake, such as forgetting a name, or a serious one, such as forgetting an important appointment, it reveals to us emotions we are trying hard to deny.

Joan, a thirty-two-year-old unmarried woman and a lawyer by profession, came for help because she had a case of severe sinusitis that would not go away though doctors told her there seemed nothing wrong with her nose. She divulged that she could not stop eating sweets, though her doctor told her she should lose twenty pounds.

"I just am unable to give up sweets," she said. "If I don't enjoy ice cream or chocolate cake once a day, I feel, 'What's the use of living?' " Then she confessed, "I overate on chocolate once again last night."

I said nothing, waiting for her to go on. After a long silence she said sadly, "When I was in my teens, every Sunday, when my father let me play a round of golf with him, we would wind up eating a huge portion of chocolate ice cream topped with fudge sauce."

She sighed, then admitted, "I guess I became addicted to sweets in this way."

I kept silent, wanting her to think some more about this important act in her life. She said reluctantly, "I thought those moments with my father as we both sat devouring the delicious ice cream were a haven."

Then she laughed and said, "I meant to say 'heaven.' "

"Perhaps those moments were both haven and heaven," I said. "And as you devour sweets today, you unconsciously think of the 'heaven' created when you were in your early teens as you had your father all to yourself. Your rival mother and two brothers were out of the picture for the moment."

She was silent, lost in thought, so I went on, "Today you devour chocolate ice cream with hot fudge sauce as you return to the early memories when there were only you and your father in your world. You must have felt like a very happy girl at those times."

In a choked voice, she said, "Yes, I had him all to myself. We laughed, we felt good after the golf game. I lived for the moment in a special world where I felt loved by the man I loved."

As we permit ourselves to acknowledge the true emotions of childhood, many of them long buried because we were ashamed of them, or frightened by them, but which constantly appear in overeating, slips of the tongue, or unconsciously hurting ourselves in accidents, we can start the emotional climb up the ladder of success to the understanding of the inner self that has caused us sadness and grief.

CHAPTER 8

THE VERY PAINFUL FAILURES

No one is exempt from failure, for "to err is human," as Alexander Pope pointed out many decades ago. Because we human beings are neither omnipotent nor well-constructed mental machines, failure is inevitable, whether it be in love, marriage, business, sports, or academia.

Failures range from those that are rather minor and relatively painless, like those we discussed in the previous chapter, to those so painful they lead to suicide, addiction to alcohol, or drugs, to depression or acting self-destructively in work or other situations and in relationships.

One of the most serious and painful failures to befall members of the human race is the committing of suicide. Each year over forty-five thousand men, women, and adolescents in our country destroy themselves. Though their motives vary, they have much in common. People who kill themselves have given up hope that life can bestow any pleasures on them. Though there are a few suicides because of terminal illness, most of those who attempt suicide are suffering from gloom, doom, and misery. All are desperately trying to cope with serious mental conflicts that they have endured for some time.

The Self-Hatred in Suicide

One of the foremost characteristics of most suicidal people is acute self-hatred. Their self-esteem is extremely low, and they have lost hope of ever regaining a positive picture of themselves or of the world.

Let us take a common type of suicide—the man or woman who is rejected by a lover. Such a person—male or female—believes life can no longer hold meaning unless the lost love is regained. If the abandonment is permanent, this very vulnerable person no longer wants to live. He has lost the essential prop that has provided the confidence necessary to continue living. For such a person, the presence of the lover or spouse is absolutely essential to sustain existence, much as an infant needs its mother in order to survive.

Those whose sense of personal worth requires a certain affluence may think of suicide as the only recourse if they lose their income. During the 1930s, after the stock market crashed, many suicides were committed by men who needed a substantial and visible income to feel worthwhile. Without their wealth they felt worthless, despondent, and deeply ashamed, as if they had committed an unforgivable crime.

The man or woman who commits suicide is usually overwhelmed by shame because of the threat of public exposure. Examples turn up in the newspapers regularly. Recently a colonel in the army, highly successful and respected by his colleagues, was reported to have been involved in a homosexual affair. Distorting the meaning of his affair and viewing it as a heinous crime, when it was exposed to public view he felt so acutely ashamed of himself that he destroyed mind and body.

In the late 1980s the *New York Times* reported the case of Barbara Watson, who in 1974 began working for the Department of Parks and Recreation in Westport, Connecticut. She was thirty-five years old, divorced, with two young daughters. Though her salary was low, somehow she managed to take care of her daughters. She was described by friends as a woman who never complained, was always cheerful and helpful.

At the Department of Parks Mrs. Watson worked her way up from clerk typist to office manager. She eventually became a deputy director, a job she held until the last five years of her life. Part of her duties was to collect greens fees at the municipal golf course, paid chiefly in cash.

Suddenly it was discovered that the records of the rounds played on the course did not correspond to the financial records for the revenues collected. More than thirty thousand dollars a year was unaccounted for in each of the last three years that Mrs. Watson had been collecting.

At first her superiors thought there must have been a clerical error. Her boss, Stuart McCarthy, the Park Department's director, maintained, "You've got to trust an employee who's been in that position fifteen years." Determined to resolve the matter, however, he suspended Mrs. Watson with pay.

Two days after the suspension, Westport police responded to a call from one of Mrs. Watson's daughters. Her mother had been found in the bedroom of her modest home, a plastic bag covering her head, dead of self-inflicted asphyxiation.

She left no note. It was presumed she had taken the money to pay for her daughters' college expenses. Family and friends were shocked and bereaved. They could not believe either that she had stolen the money or that she had killed herself.

Shame seemed the dominant motive in Barbara Watson's suicide. She feared her embezzlement would be revealed and hated herself for being known as a thief who would certainly lose her job and her reputation. She could not tolerate the shame of facing prison or at least being viewed as a criminal.

In trying to understand the low self-esteem and overwhelming feelings of shame that are part and parcel of suicide, we have to realize that the self-loathing and the acute shame often have little to do with reality. When the actress Marilyn Monroe killed herself by overdosing on barbiturates, she was highly successful, beautiful, and esteemed by almost every man in the world.

Though many books have been written about Marilyn, little is known of the cruel background that led to such an inner hatred that at the age of thirty-six she committed suicide. The fears and terrors of her very early life, lacking both a father and mother, growing up in the home of foster parents who gave her little or no love, pervaded her existence until she could bear it no longer. Alcohol and pills during the years of success only increased her mental agony. She did not trust (could not love) man or woman and eventually turned the hate on herself.

Similarly, Barbara Watson hated herself for not being able to pay for her daughters' education, as well as hating herself for stealing money. While the latter is a crime, in her case far from an impulsive crime, it did not warrant the enormity of the self-hatred that led to suicide. Very often, though not always, the person who commits suicide is loved by many who are sympathetic to the plight that led him to destroy himself. Almost always the suicidal person is his own worst enemy.

The Many Faces of Suicide

Perhaps one of the least understood facets of suicide is that the person who commits it lives in an acute rage, a rage that is usually buried very deep before it explodes. Frequently those who kill themselves have held murderous wishes toward some one or ones who have frustrated or rejected them. But suicidal people also hate themselves for their murderous wishes, remembering the commandment "Thou shalt not kill." They are very much in the position of children who feel they are unworthy because they hate their parents and therefore must punish themselves by believing they are not fit to live.

Of the two types of individuals who tend to commit suicide, one has been reared in an atmosphere of emotional deprivation that verges on cruelty—deserted by parents or brought up by uncaring parents who, because of the way *their* parents treated them as children, could not be warm and loving. The hatred the child feels toward uncaring parents, intolerable as it is, cannot be articulated because to speak of it is to risk total abandonment. Such a child reasons that cruel parents are better than none but nonetheless feels guilty. Some children, believing they are unloved, possessing no outlet to discharge their anger and hatred, turn that hatred on themselves and, instead of thinking about murdering their parents, murder themselves instead.

It appears that some murderers like themselves more than they like their parents and feel a certain justification in killing them. Other murderers start to suffer acute loss of self-esteem, shame, and despondency, and eventually do commit suicide. Taking a perverse view of this issue, we could say that a murderer such as Willie Bosket, Jr., who shot two men dead in a subway and almost killed a guard in the prison to which he was sent, possessed more self-esteem than a suicidal person such as Marilyn Monroe.

There is a second type of suicidal person, one whose life story is quite different from those described above. This second type has usually been the recipient of a certain degree of love, success, and attention. But he can love himself only if he keeps receiving attention, love, and visible signs of success. Why is this so?

The suicidal son who needs to have his self-confidence and self-esteem constantly refueled has usually lived in a home where his parents showed him a love that was intermittent and conditional. He received love only when he gave his parents what they insisted on receiving from him—high grades in school, a good batting average on the ball field, a stirring performance in the high school play. The suicidal daughter may have had to excel in school or win a beauty contest or triumph in other traditionally female activities.

Conditional love is referred to by child psychologists as emotional blackmail. The child is not loved for himself but only when he fully satisfies his parents' ambitions for him. We might call it emotional rape. The child lives in a rage because the parental love and attention depends so much on total submission to the egocentric and arbitrary demands of the parents. Although only dimly aware of it, the child needs and wants to be loved for just being.

Usually the parents we describe treat their children as they were treated by their own parents when they were children. Little children and big children all identify with their parents, regardless of how immature and insensitive the parents' behavior may be. For many years and for virtually all children in all cultures, parents are the role models and their rules and regulations, values and idiosyncrasies, no matter how arbitrary or absurd, are like Supreme Court decisions and Constitutional mandates to their children. This is why child abuse can be seen in three or more family generations of parent-child relationships, as love and cooperation can be apparent through other family generations of parents and their children.

When a child is loved conditionally, such as only on those occasions when he accomplishes athletic or intellectual feats, he looks for those same conditions in adult life to bring him love and admiration. A good example of this repetition in adult life of what occurred in childhood can be found in the life of Ernest Hemingway. As a child Hemingway was loved if he produced brilliant statements for his parents to enjoy. For a while he felt loved as an adult, producing written gems for society. However, when the amount of success, attention, and love for which he yearned was not forthcoming in the amount he craved he committed suicide.

The adult who as a child was emotionally blackmailed and emotionally raped hates himself if he thinks he is not satisfying others. If he fails at a task, he feels unworthy and is sure he deserves punishment. We might view suicide as the most extreme form of self-punishment by an individual who believes himself despicable and not worthy of living.

As strongly and as frequently as we have referred to the self-hatred of the suicidal person, it is also important to reiterate that hating oneself starts with hatred toward another person. The scream of a baby tells of his rage toward the parent who is frustrating him. As he grows, the youngster may vent this anger in words.

It is only when the child does not feel safe in asserting himself, out of a fear of censure and punishment, that he begins to find hateful feelings intolerable and then turns these feelings against himself.

The murderous feelings of the suicidal person surface frequently in suicide notes. These notes are attempts to punish those the suicidal person hates—those he believes have driven an emotional dagger through his heart. One rejected husband wrote in a suicide note to his wife, "I love you always. I'm sorry you couldn't return my love. This is my only way out."

The intense rage in this husband is obvious when he implies his wife caused his suicide because she could not love him the way he wanted her to. When a man commits suicide and blames his wife, he is probably blaming the first woman in his life as well—his mother, perhaps also a grandmother or a sister, from whom he felt not love but hatred. The same phenomenon occurs with women who commit suicide, accusing their husbands indirectly of being the cause of their death. These women in most cases hated their fathers and other men in their lives.

The suicidal person—whether man or woman—lives with a harsh self-evaluation and consequently always expects to be punished. Either the product of punitive parents or a parental love that was conditional, these men and women cannot truly like themselves because they were never loved for themselves alone. They are furious at the cruelties they have endured. They would secretly like to break every rule, every parental mandate inflicted on them. But this desire leads to self-hatred and a conviction that they deserve the severest punishment. *They* are now cruel because of their rebellious wishes, and must be wiped out for possessing such wishes.

What Depression Tells Us

One expression of painful failure is depression. Thousands of men, women, and children are severely depressed but their depression often goes unrecognized. Instead, they are regarded as chronic underachievers, tired men and women, moody children, and hypochondriacs.

Inasmuch as most of us feel depressed from time to time it is important to understand how and why we become depressed. When attributes of ours that we consider important to the image we wish to convey to the world and to ourselves are demeaned or derogated, we get angry. Unless we are able to acknowledge and accept our anger at the person who has berated us, we will become depressed. When we are depressed we beat up on ourselves, identify with our critics, legitimize their complaints toward us, and feel like guilty children. Depression is often a substitute for legitimate and honest anger.

Depression can also result when we feel we have lost somebody or something essential in our lives. When we lose family members, close friends, lovers, jobs, status, or prized possessions such as expensive jewelry or a new car, we often find it difficult to acknowledge and accept our indignation. Instead, we again deny our anger, turn ourselves into sad children, and feel we cannot be or should not be loved. When we are depressed, we feel like a deprived child instead of an adult who has a right to experience resentment.

As Judith Viorst pointed out in her book *Necessary Losses*, we have a right to be annoyed when we experience losses. We do not have to blame ourselves for them; they happen to everyone, and none of us should feel compelled to like them.

Many of us react with depression when we cannot have our own way. We want to attack those who we feel hinder us from achieving our desires or who do not appreciate our capabilities. However, in lieu of permitting ourselves to feel a natural resentment, we turn our anger against ourselves and think, "I don't amount to much or I would be loved far more, noticed far more, and admired far more."

If we expect love to be constant and admiration to be ever-present, we are doomed to unending depression. The depressed person is usually a very narcissistic person who wants to be in the limelight constantly. When the limelight does not shine, these men and women first fall into a rage. But their depression emerges when they begin to feel sorry for themselves. They cannot accept that life is full of frustrations and necessary losses. Their gloom and doom is an expression of their inability to accept reality as it is. They long for the lost paradise that never existed.

Chronically depressed people who need others to gratify their wishes twenty-four hours a day include the cranky spouse, the sulky child, and the withdrawn friend. Such people never feel too sure of themselves. As children they never felt consistently loved and trusted by their parents or others. For some, the rejection was real and their parents *were* hateful. Others, whose parents were indulgent, never learned to take no for an answer. They lived constantly collecting injustices, furious that others did not create the Garden of Eden and the paradise they feel is their proper due.

Psychoanalyst Roy Schafer has defined self-esteem as

reasonable confidence in the self. If we do not possess a reasonable amount of reasonable confidence, we will feel depressed. When we do not like ourselves sufficiently, we seek for others to fill our emotional vacuums. When they do not help us, which is inevitable, we feel angry and then depressed.

The Meaning of Masochism

Often existing side by side with depression, as we feel sadness, loss, and low self-esteem, masochism, another type of painful failure, may take over. In a state of masochism we undergo physical or emotional pain from which we allow ourselves to feel some pleasure.

The masochistic man, woman, or child does not feel entitled to pleasure. His conscience—the voices of his internalized parents—forbids him to enjoy life. He must suffer while receiving pleasure or endure pain before the pleasure and perhaps afterwards as well.

For example, many men and women can enjoy sex only if they have a heated and painful argument before or after the sexual act. An extreme form of masochism occurs when men or women are whipped or physically hurt during sex. They cannot enjoy sexual pleasures unless they are severely punished for it.

When we have punitive consciences, we seek penalties and punishments to ease our tensions. As noted in previous chapters, many failures in business, sports, academia, love, marriage, and in parent-child relationships are no more and no less than a means of punishing ourselves for the success and pleasure we strongly desire but which we feel too guilty to enjoy.

The masochistic person feels that he is an evil sinner

and should be severely admonished and punished for his wrongdoing. If he is not suffering in the present he awaits the axe that will fall in the future. The characters created by Dostoyevski and Tolstoy are poignant examples of masochists, frequently burdening themselves with pain and misery in a fervent desire to expiate their sins. If others do not berate them, they berate themselves. To feel relaxed or fulfilled is equivalent in their minds to committing a crime. And they believe a crime always deserves a punishment!

The masochistic person—man, woman, or child—usually experiences pain silently but secretly hopes his sufferings will be admired. He turns the other cheek in pain but really hopes he will be admired for his deep anguish. Often overlooked in masochism is the exhibitionism that is part of it. The masochistic person consistently bellows, "You must look at me and commiserate with me because I am in enormous pain."

In every masochistic person resides a martyrdom. As the masochist suffers humiliation and endures pain, he feels a sense of virtue and pride. This explains why he will submit for many years to a grumbling boss, a torturing spouse, an unfaithful lover, or a sadistic mother-in-law. The masochist's unconscious wish to suffer explains why people habitually frequent offices of sadistic lawyers, temperamental dentists, arrogant physicians, and incompetent psychotherapists. As he feels tortured, the masochist enjoys a temporary ease of tension.

Dr. Theodor Reik in *Masochism in Modern Man* said poignantly, describing the masochist, "The lambskin he wears, hides a wolf. His yielding includes defiance, his submissiveness, opposition. Beneath his softness there is hardness; behind the obsequiousness rebellion is concealed."

In effect, Reik uncovered the hatred and sadism that

exists in every masochist. It is a hatred and sadism that he persists in keeping as a secret from others but, most important, from himself.

Dr. Shirley Pankin in her book *The Joy of Suffering* wrote of the "sweet revenge" in masochism. She demonstrated that inherent in masochism is hidden pleasure, pointing out that for many centuries women, supposedly more masochistic than men, were forced to be subservient. Physical illness and psychological suffering were the main ways women could take a partial but pleasurable revenge on men. It is reasonable to suggest that as women achieve more equality with men their masochism will diminish. When they feel as worthwhile as men, women will not then feel compelled or coerced into victimized roles.

The psychiatrist, Dr. John MacGregor, has pointed out that masochistic people always move toward enacting the role of victim. Rather than face their destructive wishes they either become victims in sadomasochistic relationships or fantasize themselves as such. When they are victims they can deny what Reik calls "the wolf" in themselves. They gain, Reik says, victory through defeat. In effect, they feel a sense of triumph over their oppressors by feeling acutely victimized.

Of Addiction, Body Ailments, and Psychosomatic Ills

Many men and women express their need to fail by becoming addicts. Although much has been written and discussed about the causes and treatment of such addictions as alcohol, drugs, gambling, and smoking, it has not been sufficiently demonstrated that all addicts are guilt-ridden people who must undergo punishment and suffering.

Every alcoholic after his binges has painful hangovers in which he demeans and derogates himself for many hours—sometimes for many days. A drug addict, after experiencing the "high" in which euphoria reigns for a while, invariably sinks to a low and becomes very depressed. A chronic gambler has strong, although unconscious, wishes to lose and never relaxes completely with his winnings. Under the guise of wanting to win even more, he inevitably loses. Although smokers get some gratification from their inhalations, they also suffer from breathing disorders, heart problems, and cancer.

Behind the hunger for alcohol and drugs, or indeed any addiction, lies the need of the addict to gratify a far earlier hunger. The addict is, in many ways, a baby yearning for a nurturing mother. Yet he denies his emotional hunger and becomes afraid of emotional intimacy; he is much too frightened to depend on others and feels suffocated if others depend on him. Because he is extremely afraid to disclose the baby he secretly wishes to be with his spouse or friends, he renounces relationships and clings to his bottle of liquor. The liquor serves as a substitute for the bottle of milk he secretly craves. He is obsessed with "Lady Luck" when he gambles rather than face how much he longs to be protected and fed by a nurturing mother. He would prefer to suck on and bite the stem of his pipe in private than to allow himself to consider how he would like to suck on or bite the nipple of a breast.

Important to all addictions is a strong feeling of emotional deprivation, after which the individual feels deep rage at those who have withheld love and support. The addict cannot cope with his fury, feels guilty for possessing it, and hates himself. To bring pleasure into his life, which he is convinced he cannot get from human beings, he resorts to the chronic use of alcohol, drugs, or other solitary means of gratification.

One way of coping with feelings that disturb us is to arrange for our bodies to express them. During the past three decades a field has arisen called psychosomatics. This is a specialization that attempts to heal those men and women who experience very painful bodily failures, such as ulcer, asthma, heart irregularities, and migraine headaches.

What those of us who work in the mental health field are learning more and more is that when we human beings cannot acknowledge painful emotions to ourselves, we convert them into painful bodily sensations. The person suffering from a psychosomatic disease buries his feelings in his unconscious and is hardly ever aware of them. But the human organism is such that no matter how deeply an emotion is buried, it will express itself, often through the body.

Mildred, a twenty-three-year-old woman, came to see me because she was suffering from severe migraine headaches. As I listened to her I quickly became aware that she was a soft-spoken person who suppressed her feelings. Early in our work she told me she was an executive secretary to a tyrannical boss.

She admitted that she always acquiesced in her boss's tyranny and acquiesced in all of his demands. When I asked how she felt about being her boss's slave, she replied, "I never considered myself a slave but a dutiful civil servant."

As I noted to myself that Mildred was holding back heaps of rage and burying her feelings during the session, I realized at the same time she was stroking her forehead.

I said, "You appear to be in some kind of pain."

She smiled politely, then said, "I have a small headache but it will go away."

I was able to help Mildred understand that she held intense feelings of dislike toward her boss, which she found it very difficult to discuss. In time she was able to describe how angry she felt toward him. She called him a tyrant and added that he reminded her of her oppressive father, to whom she had always submitted as a child. When Mildred was able to air her buried resentments in my office, she became comfortable in her own office, and her headaches eventually disappeared.

Although many different causes are attributed to the very painful headache, such as brain irregularities, hormonal dysfunctions, and heredity, it seems quite clear that when we have aching thoughts spinning in our heads which cannot be discharged, a migraine headache often is a result.

Frequently when my patients in psychotherapy complain of an ache in a particular zone of the body, such as the stomach, I will ask, "What is your stomach saying?"

Most patients welcome this question and frequently are able to air the feelings that have caused upset stomach. Fred, age forty, came to see me because he had been suffering from ulcers for fifteen years. They started when he entered military service, but he had never found out what it was about the military setting that precipitated his painful malady.

One day during a therapeutic session with me, Fred began to talk about how deeply he had missed his home while in the army and how much he resented sergeants and his other superiors. While reminiscing about the army, he told me that his stomach was growling and he felt an ulcer attack coming on.

I asked him, "What do you suppose your stomach is saying about your experiences in the army?"

Not realizing his choice of words, Fred bellowed, "I could never stomach the army!"

He then added, "I had to swallow shit and take a lot of crap from too many people. The whole thing was very distasteful and I had to keep swallowing the junk!"

When Fred could more and more realize that he yearned for a good mother instead of a bellowing sergeant, but could not admit this to himself nor tell anyone else how he felt, he started to feel a sense of relief. Like most people who develop ulcers he suffered from deep dependency yearnings he could not tolerate. In the army he swallowed "crap" when he really pined for warm milk from a nurturing mother.

Incidentally, those of us who work with patients who suffer from psychosomatic ills have found that the best way to begin the healing process of an ulcerative attack is to give the patient a glass of milk accompanied by a warm smile.

I have seen many men and women become free of their stomach ulcers when they could verbalize their wishes to be given to and freer to admit their anger when frustrated. In our society it is less acceptable for men to acknowledge their dependency wishes. Consequently, many men bury these wishes, which explains why more men than women suffer from stomach ulcers.

Because the body expresses many of our psychological ills, there are different types of psychosomatic problems. A very common one is insomnia. Thousands of men and women do not receive sufficient rest during the night because they are busy planning the next day or are still caught up in the complications of the day just past. Many times the person with insomnia is not able to "get away from it all," as we are supposed to do when we go on vacation or go to bed at night.

To sleep is to permit ourselves to go on a vacation. It is a healthy and adaptive regression to a state that all of us should allow ourselves to enjoy. But to sleep, we have to be able to say good-bye to those persons with whom we had transactions during the day and postpone greeting and conversing with those we plan to see tomorrow. This requires an ability to stop working and still like ourselves as we do so. If we feel too much anger, too much guilt, or too much self-consciousness, we may develop insomnia.

Robert, fifteen years old, who was referred to me for counseling, suffered from insomnia. I was able to help him overcome the insomnia when he could eventually share with me the constant worrying he endured about excelling in football games.

He felt so pressured to throw long forward passes, make extraordinary punts, and be an all-star in each game that he could not say good night to his football. He vicariously played long football games in bed instead of sleeping. After I helped him lower his expectation of being the world's greatest football player, he eventually got his much-needed rest.

Most insomniacs are driven individuals who feel they must accomplish superhuman feats. Their minds are extremely active as they obsess about how they are going to write the great American novel, beat Babe Ruth's total of home runs hit in a season, or make a million dollars quickly. They are busy at work trying to achieve all night as well as all day.

The Grip of Phobias and Obsessions

In any discussion of very painful failures, our phobias, obsessions and compulsions should not be overlooked.

Many people suffer from such phobias as fear of the dark, fear of being trapped in elevators, fear of flying. When we are gripped by a phobia we feel in danger of suffering from some hidden guilt, perhaps even fear dying on the spot.

If somebody fears the dark, he is often afraid he will be attacked because he deserves punishment for some forbidden wish or wishes. June, thirteen years old, was deathly afraid of the dark. She kept her bedroom dimly lit all night. Her parents did not realize, nor was June aware, that the darkness stirred up her forbidden sexual fantasies. When she could share some of the fantasies with me and discuss her wish to masturbate in the darkness as she imagined Prince Charming making love to her, her phobia receded. On becoming more sexually enlightened, she no longer had to keep her light on during the night.

Jack, a twenty-two-year-old athlete, sought my help because he feared to fly. This fear was about to cost him his job inasmuch as traveling on an airplane was a constant requirement in his work as a professional hockey player. When Jack could admit his forbidden wishes to soar, to surpass all the athletes in creation and to look down on them from on high, he could slowly accept the reality of flying. The more he could accept his soaring fantasies and realize they were wishes that hurt no one, the more he could relax in peace on the airplane.

Forbidden wishes often lie at the bottom of obsessions and compulsions. The compulsion to constantly clean one's hands or the house is a way of warding off thoughts and wishes to be "dirty." The compulsion almost every child possesses when he walks on the sidewalk is the fear of stepping on a crack. The childish refrain goes, "If you step on a crack, you break your mother's back." The forbidden wish is the child's anger toward his mother, which he cannot openly express. By avoiding stepping on cracks he magically avoids facing his destructive feelings toward his mother.

When a child or adult enacts a compulsion, he is trying very hard to wipe out a forbidden wish. The compulsive cleaner tries to erase from his mind wishes to play with dirt. The compulsive workhorse is trying to avoid his wishes to be lazy and to do nothing. The compulsive sexual addict is trying to deny a deep sexual paralysis.

To overcome an obsession or a compulsion we have to be kinder to ourselves. We have to give ourselves permission to want to play with dirt, to be idle or sexually promiscuous. We also have to remind ourselves occasionally that *to wish* to do something differs mightily from doing it.

Those who suffer from phobias, compulsions, and psychosomatic ills as well as masochism, depression, and suicidal wishes, all possess extremely punitive consciences, or what therapists call superegos. Those who have to cope with painful failures have frequently, if not always, been loved only conditionally.

They have had to produce, in many cases, what their parents wanted them to produce, not what came naturally. They were permitted to admit only certain feelings and ideas and had to deny the existence of those that were "wrong," such as the sexual ones or the aggressive ones that might harm those persons they disliked or even hated.

Thus they grew up worrying about the axe that would befall them if they disobeyed any law laid down by a mother or father. Often they could only stay alive, they believed, if they felt punished or abused because of a fleeting angry or sexual thought.

In contrast to most of the failures discussed throughout this book, those who experience the very painful ones described in this chapter may need counseling or psychotherapy. It is difficult to overcome extreme anguish by oneself. Reading of ways to do this is the starting point for many, who then seek help to delve even further into the early miasma of confusion that had such a deep and deleterious impact on their ability to function as happy and productive human beings.

CHAPTER 9

SUCCESSFUL TREATMENT OF TWO PSYCHOLOGICAL FAILURES

Many times I have been asked, "What kinds of people come to you for psychotherapy?" After practicing the profession for close to forty years I can now answer the question with relative certainty.

People who seek psychotherapy are usually the more courageous, the more mature, and the more responsible members of society. After trying to blame others for their failures, as we all tend to do to some extent, these are the ones willing to face themselves and at long last recognize that overcoming misery and unhappiness in love and work rests primarily within themselves.

I have often been asked to describe the psychotherapeutic process—to show the uninitiated and uninformed just what transpires between therapist and patient. In this chapter I will review my therapeutic work with two people who were failing in many areas of life and who responded well to my help. I hope that my description of their therapy will not only familiarize the reader with some of the features of psychotherapy but help him apply to himself, if he feels the need, some of the issues in my work with these two patients. I had to help them realize there is no such thing as perfection. To be comfortable with yourself means you accept your imperfections, your right to be wrong occasionally.

The two cases were very different. In the first case Jack, a college dropout, discovered that his failures were largely due to unrealistic ambitions emanating from a childhood of overindulgence. The second case involved a young woman, Diane who, by contrast, had been neglected and deprived and who as a growing child now faced the world as if all its inhabitants were her sick, depressed mother.

The College Dropout

I first met Jack, a nineteen-year-old young man, when he was referred to me after failing most of his courses in his freshman year at Columbia University. The guidance personnel of the University suggested that Jack take a year off from college and seek treatment; they recommended that when the therapist advised the college that Jack was psychologically able to return, he could do so.

I now learned from this tall, attractive, well-dressed young man that he daydreamed incessantly, attended porno films almost daily, masturbated compulsively, was often on drugs, and at times felt deeply depressed.

His relationship with people consisted of a weekly chat with his father, who gave him a more than adequate allowance of $150 a week in addition to an apartment for which his father paid. Jack told me he visited call girls and prostitutes when he felt the urge, saying he had never really fallen in love with a girl. "Can't trust them," he said in his first interview.

He mentioned that the Dean of Students had referred him to me because "he thought my work wasn't satisfactory." He boasted that he had been teacher's pet in both grammar and high schools. But now that he found himself a miniscule part of a large metropolitan university where nobody gave him much attention, he had little desire to study.

Jack's history revealed that throughout his life he had felt he was everyone's favorite. His mother loved him without reservation. As an only child he was not only adored and doted upon by both parents but his grandmother, grandfather, uncles, and aunts all thought, according to Jack, that he was "terrific."

After answering some of my questions about his current life and history, he attempted in this first interview to manipulate me. He assured me, "I know full well that I can do college work." Then added, rather truculently, "If you will write a letter right away, saying I am capable of doing college work, I'm sure I can and everything will be ironed out."

One of the ways a therapist learns about his patient's conflicts and how to help him resolve them is by observing carefully how the patient acts with him. A self-effacing person will readily become a self-effacing patient, demeaning himself over and over very early in the therapeutic contact. A demanding, clinging person will relate to the therapist the same way he relates to other persons—he will be demanding and clinging. This phenomenon is known as transference. He transfers to the therapist the feelings he held toward former people important to his life, primarily his mother and father.

Thus during therapy patients ascribe to the therapist all the qualities they experienced in their parents and in other important individuals in their life such as nurses, grandparents, aunts, and uncles. As the patient learns how and why he relates the way he does to the therapist, he begins to better understand the child within and how this child first arranged and still arranges for current failures.

In demanding that I get him out of trouble immediately, Jack showed little desire to assume responsibility for himself. Like a helpless infant, he wanted me to take over and negotiate his life for him. I knew almost immediately that if I were to gratify his request, I would become the indulgent mother or father who promoted Jack's infantile behavior. It would be like giving the breast to an infant who needed to be weaned.

Jack was in for a dose of frustration. After he had belligerently demanded that I write the required letter, much as a sergeant commands a private, I asked, "How can either of us be sure that you're ready to return to college so quickly?"

Jack looked at me sullenly and retreated into silence. I, too, chose silence, telling myself that Jack no doubt manipulated others by giving them the same silent treatment when they did not do what he requested. Realizing that Jack's sullenness and silence was another attempt to manipulate me into action and knowing it would not be constructive to respond to his manipulations, I continued to join him in silence.

After about five quiet minutes he attacked me verbally, bellowing, "You are supposed to help people, not hurt them. Are all shrinks sadists like you? If I were a therapist I'd treat my patients with kindness. I would have written that letter. Don't you have a heart?"

For the remainder of the first session Jack continued to

attack me. He threatened not to return, though he undoubtedly realized that if he did not get a letter from me to the authorities at the University, he would be powerless to change his situation. At any rate, toward the end of the interview he tried a new tactic. He turned conciliatory and said, "Look, Dr. Strean, I realize you may not have thought my situation through carefully enough. I'm a competent student. I can return to college and function well enough to pass all the exams. You're entitled to make some mistakes because you don't know me very well. Think it over and maybe you'll have the letter next time we meet."

When I met Jack for his second interview he immediately asked, "Can I have the letter?"

I told him, "I have not written a letter."

In what would be his characteristic way of dealing with frustration in therapy, Jack first threw a temper tantrum, then sunk into depression.

"You really are a cruel man, Dr. Strean," he finally said accusingly. "You don't want me as a patient. I thought therapists were supposed to help not hinder those who seek some sort of aid. Don't you want to build my self-confidence?" Then a plea, "Come on, give me a letter. Let me return to the University. I'll be off your back and you'll be off mine."

To respond to Jack's temper tantrum in any way would have been unhelpful to him. This young man was failing in college because his manipulative machinations were not working. To permit him to control me via temper tantrums would actually be unkind and unwise—hardly what I would call giving him help. Therefore I kept quiet. When Jack realized his ranting and raving brought no words from me, he seemed to fall into an extreme depression. His eyes filled with tears, he wiped them away pathetically, then tried once more to convince me and himself how deeply deprived and misunderstood he was and what a torturous man I had turned out to be.

His behavior meant a difficult time for a therapist. Tears of a patient, regardless of their reason, move us. It takes arduous work and much discipline to determine the patient's motives for crying. When these motives become clear, the therapist knows how to respond in the most constructive way.

Tears may stem from deep hurt, acute loss, agony, desperation, pain of all degrees. But tears are occasionally used to elicit a response, and this, I thought, is what Jack hoped to accomplish. Though he felt in pain because I did not gratify his request, he was using tears primarily to soften my firm position.

Jack soon realized that neither temper tantrums nor crying jags would persuade me to write a letter to the University officials recommending his immediate reinstatement. Nonetheless he used these two ways of coping for the next several weeks. He was not a young man to give up easily.

Occasionally he changed the subject to talk about his loneliness and depression in day-to-day life. One morning he said, as though it were an indisputable fact, "There's nobody out there I can love or trust. Everybody's for himself." Then he returned to the plea that I write the all-important letter.

His statement about nobody to love or trust referred to me as he experienced my attitude and thoughts and it applied to Jack himself, who did not appear particularly lovable or trustworthy. Basically he acted like a baby who sought the eternal breast. If he received the milk, he would recover from temper tantrums and depression.

The letter he wanted from me was the equivalent of a breast that he demanded be given to him pronto, whereas I in effect wanted to act like a mature parent and wean a baby who should be more than ready for the experience of maturing. But he kept trying to persuade me to be the indulgent mother as he alternated between the temper tantrums that grew progressively more intense and a sadness that at times made him seem suicidal.

Suicidal threats must be understood and evaluated very carefully by the therapist so that an actual suicide can be avoided. When someone cannot eat or sleep, shows limited emotion, dresses in a disheveled way, or threatens to kill himself, he should be taken seriously when he appears severely depressed. However, since Jack was also eating and sleeping, appeared well-dressed, showed a wide range of emotions, a therapist could be fairly certain his suicidal threats were attempts to frighten the therapist into becoming the feeding mother whom the patient was demanding.

To make the distinction takes experience and understanding. One of the best barometers a therapist uses is his own feelings and reactions as he silently studies them both in the company of the patient and between the sessions. I found myself at times feeling mildly amused by Jack as he struggled with me. I knew he wished to return to the University; a part of him clearly wanted to succeed in college. I also knew he was reluctant to work. All his life he had used his native endowment to clear an easy path when anything came up that he wished to do.

With Jack I felt in many ways like a loving father who cared about his wayward son. I thought I could help him succeed if I disciplined myself not to yield to his childish demands, for to do so could only hurt him further, keep him from becoming adult.

Jack finally realized that neither temper tantrums nor depression would change my mind about the letter and that his threats of suicide did not alarm me. One day when he tried once again to scare me with suicide threats, I asked, "Where do you plan to commit suicide?"

He looked baffled by my unexpected question and immediately changed the subject. I had shown him I was not unduly alarmed. He gave up the threat for the moment, tried a new tactic.

After three months of therapy during which he continually tried to give me orders, one day he said in a conciliatory tone, "I really don't think you understand me too well, Dr. Strean. There are very moody, unhappy people who need giving adults. You are not a giving person and you're going to fail with me as a psychologist."

Jack was displaying one of the major motives in academic failure, perhaps in other failures too. He was willing to have his therapy destroyed and possibly prevent himself from returning to the University if he could defeat me. Many men and women who fail are gratifying their revengeful fantasies. By their failures they hurt parents, teachers, and therapists. Some may even go so far as to commit suicide in protest against the therapists they have chosen, who are just like their ungiving parents and others in their past who have deprived them in any way.

Actually, a turning point in Jack's therapy involved a discussion of a possible suicide. During the fifth month of his twice-a-week visits, as he continued to insist that I was a miserable fellow who offered no release from his pain, he said, "Suicide is the only way out and I'm going to do it tonight."

I asked, "Before or after supper?"

He looked at me as if trying to control his feelings, then giggled, obviously amused by my remark. Then he said,

"You really don't let me get away with anything, do you? You're like a father who doesn't allow me to kick you around." He added, thoughtfully, "Sometimes I even like you."

This was the turning point. Jack started to talk about his mother and father. He said he realized that their continued indulgence had not always helped him accept reality. "I didn't realize until I met you," he added, "that while my mother and father meant well, they were always scared to say no to me and I knew I could get away with anything."

It took Jack several more months to reach other significant conclusions. He realized he was trying to be a little prince at college but "it didn't work like it seemed to work at home and in high school," he confessed.

When I became aware that his grandiose fantasies were losing their power as he stopped acting like a baby entitled to demand constant feeding, I knew that Jack had started to function more as a young man. I was quite sure he would now participate as a member of the human race, feeling less like a baby and less like a prince.

During his seventh month of therapy, he took a part-time job as a salesman in a clothing store and also enrolled in three courses in a community college—biology, literature, and psychology. He had become interested in understanding the vagaries of the human mind, for which I both took credit and gave thanks.

He did reasonably well on the job and in his college courses but after several weeks started to feel depressed again. He threatened to quit the job, college, *and* therapy. He told me, "In all three places I feel very unappreciated." Then he started to blast me, "You have the most unsympathetic attitude in the world. I'm trying hard to do well and all you want to do is to understand me. You never praise me."

I listened quietly, saying to myself that a therapist comes to his office not to praise his patient but to understand him. I used my silent thought to help Jack as I said, "You know you have been doing quite well at college, on the job and in therapy. But you're the kind of guy who needs help by not being admired so much. You've had enough of that from your parents. In a way it's crippling."

Jack protested at first, then on further reflection repeated what he had confessed a few months previously. "You're trying to be an old man to me and make me your kid. I see now you're a different kind of old man than my father." He paused, then added, "Okay, don't admire me. I'll admire myself."

At these words from Jack, I realized he was on the right track. If he could like himself for work well done and didn't need constant pats on the back, I knew he was on the road to maturity and starting to climb the ladder of success.

It is important to note that whether you are in psychotherapy, as Jack was, or in any other learning situation, resolving failure is never a smooth process. Jack fought hard against changing his childish ways, as all of us do. Then he tried something new. In his case it meant giving up, without feeling frustrated, some of his grandiosity, his wish to have what he wanted at the moment he wanted it. This is how a baby feels, not an adult.

However, whether it is a breast, a bottle, an addiction, or a self-destructive relationship, giving up anything is never easy. We take one step forward but two steps backward. Whether we are a teacher or a student, a patient in therapy or a therapist, a self-taught student or a self-taught patient, learning and growth never move at a steady, consistent pace.

Following his ninth month of therapy Jack openly acknowledged that our work was having an impact. He now could admit, "All my life I was given in to by everybody, loved it, and didn't realize that as you get older you do have responsibilities to others."

As Jack became able to think of others, he began to read all he could find in books and articles about psychology. He even purchased one of my books—a high tribute. He also began to examine his relationship to adults and peers more seriously. He produced one vignette after another to substantiate the notion that he had never considered alternatives other than one single possibility—that he be allowed to reign as His Highness the Prince.

With his increased ability to renounce some of his pomposity, Jack was able to finish a successful semester at the community college and continue his job as a salesman. Then, on his own, with little discussion, he returned to Columbia University to resume his studies. His guidance counselors had observed such a dramatic change in him after his one year of "sabbatical" that they now did not even require a letter from me. His request to return was made in such a mature manner that he did not need any proof he was now University material.

On returning full-time to his first collegiate love, Jack achieved *A*s and *B*s in all his courses. From a near-recluse, he started to date young women at the college and elsewhere. From a student who had contempt for his professors, he began to enjoy them as well as the content of the courses. From a depressed boy, he slowly became a spontaneous and warm young adult.

Jack arrived at my office for a follow-up interview three years after his treatment ended. He was about to receive his Ph.D. in philosophy; he was planning to marry and teach philosophy part-time in another well-known university.

How did therapy help Jack? As is true in most therapies, the relationship Jack developed with the therapist was the ingredient in helping him modify his destructive and self-destructive attitudes. His history was one in which his infantilism was fostered excessively by his parents and others. He never was taught that limits, frustration, and occasionally taking no for an answer were part of life.

It had been my job to teach him that a no once in a while was a valuable lesson to learn, that life at times may be full of no's. Jack had needed a parental figure to say no to him in an atmosphere of understanding, a parental figure who would not feel guilty at saying no. Though Jack balked for several months as I tried to teach him a new way of coping with life's demands, he eventually identified with my more realistic approach to living. Why could he change?

Little children, if left to their own devices in a cafeteria will, over time, choose the food they need—a diet with the proper vitamins and carbohydrates. I believe that all human beings thrive on an emotional diet that is healthy for them.

On some level Jack intuitively knew he needed to be weaned from the all-giving breast, just as babies give signs when they are ready for a bottle or glass. And just as toddlers give signs when they are ready to seek toilet training, Jack gave me signs that he needed help in restraining his wish to urinate and defecate all over the world in an indiscriminate manner.

In other words, Jack welcomed an attitude in which he was helped to tame his impulsiveness, to control his narcissism, and to learn that by trying to manipulate people, at best he would be king for a day, never for a lifetime.

We might ask if Jack could have been helped without psychotherapy. Probably not, unless he found someone he respected deeply, from whom he could take no for an answer, as he did eventually in my office. This meant he had also learned to trust me, learn from me, accept my guidance.

Many people do not necessarily need psychotherapy if they can teach themselves that life is not a Garden of Eden, that bliss at best is a momentary affair. Many, like Jack at the start of treatment, have never learned to cope with frustration and instead try to manipulate others through threats and theatrical tears.

It is possible to teach ourselves that life can be more enjoyable and productive if we limit our demands on others, empathize more with others. Jack needed psychotherapy in order to feel this way, but many of us are able to achieve similar results as we understand the infant in ourselves who never completely leaves us but whom we can finally control as we head toward greater maturity.

The Depressed Teacher

Diane first sought help when she was a single, thirty-year-old woman teaching emotionally disturbed children. An attractive woman with deep brown eyes and short blond hair, her clothes were somewhat drab, tending to reflect what would turn out to be her overall depressed attitude. Almost every patient who seeks psychotherapy shows some measure of depression, but Diane seemed acutely depressed. I could sense this as soon as I greeted her.

She explained that she sought my help because she suffered from severe bouts of depression in which she felt worthless, as well as psychosomatic ailments including migraine headaches, asthma and pervasive aches all over her body. She also confessed that she had unsatisfactory relations with most people, particularly men.

She sought therapy, she explained, because she felt "miserable too much of the time in almost every dimension of living." Most significant, I thought, was the fact that Diane's mother died when her daughter was only three years old. The one time Diane smiled in her first interview occurred when she talked about her life prior to her mother's death. I thought she was going to tell me that those three years of mothering were very valuable. But what she said, to my deep surprise, was "Daddy and I were like lovers and I was in heaven. Mother was sick most of the time and I don't really remember her very much."

Diane's smile was short-lived, perhaps like those three years of her mother's presence. She told me, too, "My mother died a few months after she gave birth to her second child, my brother." Diane further remarked in this first interview that she was described by her father and other relatives after the death of her mother as "paralyzed, depressed, with a skin that looked green, for many years."

Although from her point of view the first three years of her life were joyful because she thought of herself as her father's own love, I thought she was underestimating the importance of her mother's live presence during that time. Even though Diane felt very close to her father, her mother was alive and part of the time at least must have influenced her daughter's mental state.

Just as Jack related to me the way he related to the important people in his life, so did Diane. In the initial phase of her three-times-a-week therapy, she considered me the all-knowing, kind father of her past.

Within three months after our first consultation Diane wore colorful clothes, smiled as she entered the office, and told me she felt far happier at work. Although she had not learned much about her inner self in this short time, why did she feel so much more alive?

Diane was experiencing what therapists refer to as the honeymoon reaction that takes place with most patients after a few months of therapy. Having the chance to say whatever comes to mind, the newcomer often feels that he has met the ideal parent, one who never judges, never criticizes, only loves to understand. While this is a distortion and exaggeration of what a therapist does, the opportunity to enjoy having another person's exclusive attention often induces in the patient the kind of bliss that honeymooners describe.

Diane experienced me as a combination of a live mother and kind father. She looked forward to her sessions with much enthusiasm. During her third month of treatment she said, "I don't feel so alone any longer. Since I've met you the world appears different. I breathe better, I eat better, I feel better and I see beauty where none existed before."

Without realizing it at first, Diane experienced herself as if she were back home again with her mother and father. One of her first dreams involved a family scene in which she was with me and my wife and had become our adopted daughter.

While just having me in her life certainly helped Diane, the bliss and excitement could not last. The ecstasy of a honeymoon slowly diminishes in intensity because the lovers start to see each other as they are, rather than as they have fantasized each other to be. The same phenomenon occurs in psychotherapy as the patient begins to realize that the therapist has a life of his own and cannot be thinking of the patient every moment. Sometimes when the therapist is away from the office, on vacation or because of an illness, and the patient is on his own once again, he realizes he is not an adopted child but only one of many patients.

Every patient, as with Jack, wants praise, encouragement, reassurance, or advice, but the therapist instead will ask, "What are you thinking?" or "How do you feel now?" The frustration such questions evoke is another way of realizing that the therapist is not a perfect, always available parent.

Diane's honeymoon came to a dramatically abrupt end when an accidental meeting occurred outside of my office. I was having lunch with a female colleague, unaware that Diane was sitting to the rear of us. She overheard me laughing and talking more freely than I ever had in our own therapy sessions.

I saw Diane briefly when I stood up to leave the table, greeted her with a hello, then walked to the door of the restaurant, following my companion.

The day following this extra-therapeutic contact she came to her regular session, threw herself on the couch, then referred immediately to seeing me in the restaurant. She complained, "You were obviously enjoying yourself—and in a way that you don't enjoy yourself with me. I wondered if you were having an affair with that woman because you sounded so flirtatious. Something you never are with me."

I kept silent and she went on, "You know I thought I liked you. But after I overheard you in the restaurant, I realized you hold back a lot from me, you bastard!"

She spent the next several sessions moaning about how wonderful I had appeared at first only to disappoint her. She had strong reactions to a situation most women would accept calmly enough, knowing I had a life outside the office. I realized that she experienced me as her father, who remarried a strange woman after her mother's death and gave his daughter far less attention from then on. In effect, I was also an extremely disloyal man.

At one session she bellowed, "How dare you love another woman more than you love me!" Before I had a reaction, even a silent one, to her outrageously possessive complaint, she went on, "That was the trouble with my father. He dangled a carrot in my face, led me to believe I would be his one and only and then married my stepmother. That bitch possessed him like that bitch did you in the restaurant. You and my father are phonies!"

Diane was expressing the classic Oedipal fantasy that a girl tends to have toward her father. She wants him all to herself and if she is in therapy will relive this yearning with the therapist. Obviously a male therapist should be careful not to be seductive with a female patient and should not give her the impression that a father figure is available. As noted in earlier chapters, a main reason for marital misery occurs when mates try to extract from each other the mothering and fathering attitudes they enjoyed in infancy. Since no spouse can fulfill this tall order, many husbands and wives remain unfulfilled and miserable.

One of the most important lessons a therapist can provide is to teach the patient that a perfect mother or father is unavailable, particularly in marriage. It was important that I keep quiet when Diane attacked me for not letting her be my "one and only." As she slowly realized I would not gratify her wish in any way nor apologize for having other women in my life, including a wife, she slowly began to consider the possibility that exclusive possession of a man was but a dream.

Facing the fact that she could not be Daddy's one and

only had helped Diane somewhat, in that she began to date men and feel more relaxed with them. Another important issue came up after she saw me in the restaurant. My sitting away from her in another corner of the restaurant revived memories and feelings connected to her dead mother.

Very few children really believe in the permanency of death and Diane was no exception. She had maintained her fantasy that some day she would be reunited with her dead mother. All she had to do was find her. Though as an adult the rational part of her knew that such reuniting was a gross impossibility, her childish fantasy lived on, as in a dream.

As Diane and I talked more about her feelings on seeing me with another woman in the restaurant, she said that it was as if she had caught a glimpse of her mother laughing, only to lose her. This was similar to what transpired over and over in her childhood and adolescence. She would think she saw her mother in a crowd, only to realize that her mother would never be within her grasp.

Much of Diane's therapy consisted of bringing out her rage, hurt, disappointment, and yearnings for her mother. Much of her depression was a result of the repressed rage that she finally expressed toward the end of the first year and throughout the second year of her treatment.

Diane's therapy made me realize once more how deeply childhood events and the way they are experienced shape our view of the world and of ourselves. Just as Jack saw a world inhabited by parents who indulged his every whim, Diane interpreted the world as a graveyard where depression, gloom, and doom reigned. I could not restore her mother nor could I be the mother she still sought. But I could encourage her to mourn her mother's death and help her discharge some of the rage she felt toward her mother for, as she had thought as a child, abandoning her. Unfortunately, most children and adults experience the premature death of a loved one as an abandonment. Even more unfortunately, part of this feeling of being abandoned is that children particularly, though many adults as well, believe they have caused it—part of the omnipotence every child feels.

Diane thought that her "love affair" with her father caused her mother to hate her and eventually to abandon her through death. She even had fantasies that the woman with whom I lunched was furious at her and somehow would get even for her taking away from her even the one moment when I had said hello.

I helped Diane understand something that all people who are depressed and anticipate punishment need to understand—that whenever we feel disaster is imminent, that is, whenever we think someone is about to act against us, we have to ask ourselves, "Who do I hate? Who do I want to kill?"

Diane eventually was able to get in touch with her wish to destroy her own mother so that she could have her father all to herself. The reason a mother's premature death is such a powerful catastrophe is that a girl's natural wishes to capture her father and destroy her mother are very intense at the age of three and four. This early love for the father fosters later love for a man outside the family. If a girl's love becomes too possessive and demanding, however, she either seeks no later love or is unable to accept for long the love of any man, feeling he will reject her as she believed her father once did.

Diane began to realize with more and more clarity that her life was so impoverished, particularly her sexual life, largely because she felt like a criminal who had destroyed her mother. The fact that her mother died made her believe something most children believe but will outgrow—wishes can kill. We give up this fantasy, one that is hard to relinquish, only when we realize our wish for omnipotence can never be fulfilled.

When Diane could feel less like a guilty killer, condemned to a life of depression, and when she could admit that her father and I were entitled to wives, slowly but surely she moved toward a life of her own. She felt more motherly toward the children she taught—"more alive with them, not like my mother, who is dead," as she said. She even yearned to be a mother. At first this wish seemed stronger than her wish to marry but during the course of therapy the latter emerged. One of the main reasons she wanted to mother was to give a child what she had missed out on in her life. She realized this loss had inspired her to enter a field where she mothered children who were emotionally disturbed, as she had been as a child.

While Diane felt much less guilty, much less hateful, and much more loving as therapy ended its third and final year, I realized that the early death of her mother would probably leave an emotional scar. In spite of it, a year after she left therapy she married a physician. Two years later she sent me a picture of her new daughter along with a picture of what appeared to be a happy family.

The question we asked about the college dropout, Jack, should be asked of Diane: Could she have been helped without psychotherapy? In her case, I would say definitely not. The very early loss of her mother and the complex relationship with her father, along with a heavy and consistent depression, would add up to too great a burden for Diane to solve all her problems by herself. She needed to share with another human being the many slings and arrows of her outrageous fortune, to paraphrase Shakespeare. She required an audience of one, someone who would listen patiently and empathetically, as a good mother or father does, to her woes. She needed to express the many hidden wishes within her relationship to me and understand which ones were possible to gratify and which were not.

There are many Dianes in this world who probably should be helped during their childhood and thus spared years of misery. All children need two parents who love and respect each other and who work together, loving and respecting their children. Unfortunately, this does not occur often in our current society, which explains why we see so many depressed, unhappy children who later become alcoholic and addictive teenagers, then violent men and women.

Though Diane's mother died when her daughter was only three, the impact of divorce, desertion, and other forms of trauma create many Dianes. Fortunately, this one could be helped at the age of thirty, but other Dianes are so distrustful they do not feel free to take their problems to a therapist.

Jack, the college dropout, and Diane, the depressed schoolteacher, are moving examples of the successful treatment of failures. Therapists sometimes fail, too, in their work, and the failure can either be a function of the limitations and emotional problems of the therapist or the unwillingness of the patient to work with the therapist.

Psychotherapy in many ways is like a marital relationship. Two people with strengths and limitations, hopes and fantasies, come together to try to make life more enjoyable and more productive for the one seeking help. Just as a happy marriage requires a great deal of cooperation from the two who are involved, so does therapy if it is to be successful. The success rate of therapy, I would judge, is perhaps a little higher than the success rate of marriage.

It is well known that some therapists do better with certain types of patients; there are also patients who do better with certain types of therapists. As with childhood, as with marriage, as with every human relationship, nothing is perfect.

CHAPTER 10

ERASING FAILURE AND ENJOYING SUCCESS

Funny thing about failure: it pushes you back to work quicker than success," says Neil Simon, Pulitzer prizewinning playwright. He knows less about failure on Broadway and in the films than just about any writer of plays and films who can be named.

Failure spurs Neil Simon on. After his play *Fools* folded, following only forty performances, he wrote three hits that became eminently successful—*Biloxi Blues, Broadway Bound* and *Brighton Beach.* No sooner did his two plays *Jake's Women* and *Actors and Actresses* become flops than he turned right around and wrote two major hits, *Promises, Promises* and *Come Blow Your Horn.*

Many men, women, teenagers, and children are like Neil Simon in that they are so determined to erase failure that they persist until they attain success. Thus some penniless men and women, chronically destitute for years, eventually do become millionaires. Athletes who never reached first base persist until they achieve the ecstasy that home-run hitters frequently enjoy. Many physically ill persons conquer their illness and emerge as healthy for many decades after being pronounced close to death by a doctor.

We can learn much from persistent people who seem like abysmal failures initially, only to emerge triumphant in their particular field of endeavor. One who turned disaster into success is Larry Holmes. At forty-one years of age this former heavyweight champion, while in the final stages of training for a comeback fight, addressed a sizeable crowd in Hollywood, Florida, in April, 1991. Holmes said, "People told me 'You'll never be heavyweight champion.' I proved them wrong. I became heavyweight champion and held the title for seven and a half years. Just because I lacked education didn't mean I couldn't be somebody. I dropped out in the seventh grade. I couldn't read well. I couldn't write well. I couldn't spell well. But I didn't let lack of education stop me."

He went on, "I'm proud to say I don't need boxing. Boxing made me rich. It got me out of the ghetto. I have a street in Easton, Pa., named after me: Larry Holmes Drive. I own a building on that land that has a courthouse in it, and that courthouse has three jail cells. Here's a guy with a seventh-grade education who used to break into cars that's now got his own three jail cells."

He held the World Boxing Council title from June 9, 1978, when he beat Ken Norton, to September 22, 1985, when he lost to Michael Spinks. He could well be proud of his unusual achievement, given his early failures in school and elsewhere.

Jackie Mason, the comic, is another man who has emerged from obscurity to become one of the most popular entertainers in the United States. Like Holmes, Mason possessed a faith in himself which never wavered. No matter how down and out he felt, he showed the persistence necessary to erase failure and establish success. He believed in his own capabilities regardless of how others felt toward him or how they might tear him down.

Mason, who specializes in Jewish wit, commented, "The Jews said I was too Jewish, the Gentiles said I wasn't Jewish enough. Now I'm a sensation, telling the same Jewish jokes that made me a failure for twenty-five years."

Mason's words tell the ultimate immigrant's story in which he had to resolve a powerful conflict. Should he continue the practice of ten generations of the Mason family, all of whom became ordained rabbis, or should he try to gratify his dreams to be in show business and achieve stardom? Working against the tide of family pressure and a punitive Jewish conscience, he sustained his belief in his talents and skills, eventually to achieve stardom.

Though Mason's pain was intense and his troubles many, he consistently demonstrated what is so necessary in attaining success—the belief in your own capacities and an unambivalent persistence.

While completing his hundredth performance on Broadway in 1990, Mason declared, "Being Number One means success and anything less is failure."

The founder of psychoanalysis, Sigmund Freud, was repudiated by his peers, sneered at by the world, and called everything from a male chauvinist to a pervert, a sex maniac, an addict. But he never lost faith in the truth of his findings and while often made a scapegoat to this day, he is considered one of history's most creative scientists. The jeers and sneers, though painful to him, as they were to Mason and Holmes, never floored him. He believed strongly in his discoveries, which were to change the lives of unhappy people throughout the world.

Regardless of the field of endeavor, whether it be sports, entertainment, or science, the successful person is a self-confident person. He learns to cope with criticism because he believes that what he seeks will eventually bring much joy to himself and to others. Focusing on the pleasure that will eventually ensue, he can cope with pain, derision, and even hatred.

Ted Williams of the Boston Red Sox, one of baseball's outstanding greats, recalled that when he arrived in Boston as an unknown rookie, he announced with the openness and innocence of a teenager, "All I want out of life is that when I walk down the street folks will say, 'There goes the greatest hitter who ever lived!' " His sentiments were similar to those of one of the greatest boxers of all time, Muhammad Ali. For close to a decade he daily announced to the world and to himself, "I am the greatest!"

Ted Williams felt confident of his prowess from the moment he entered the baseball field and he was consistently successful at bat. He did not have to overcome the odds of a Larry Holmes, of a Jackie Mason, or of a Sigmund Freud. He scarcely ever encountered failure. But almost all human beings are vulnerable, and few of us have the fortune and the skills of a Ted Williams. We have to work hard to be successful. This means that we have to accept for long periods frustration, rejection, and criticism.

In overcoming failures we have to try to diminish our hatred toward those who oppose us, envy us, or reject us. The successful person, if he is to sustain his success, cannot waste his energy on fighting ferociously. His efforts and energy should be focused not on enemies, though inevitably there will be some, but on his own progress.

Unfortunately, many a potentially successful man or woman in a profession, in sports, or in the field of entertainment has been so intent on destroying his antagonists and competitors that he has not been able to concentrate on his own work. He wastes valuable time and energy that could be spent on tackling what he knows he does best, regardless of what an enemy may say or do.

Freud, though possessing enemies all of his life, was always quite loving toward his wife, children, and many, if not most, of his colleagues. Henry Aaron, the well-known baseball player, was a family man who showed much affection toward children and virtually everyone else he knew. This is not to deny that there are successful people who are capable of demonstrating hatred. However, when they do not monitor their hatred and put their energy into love of others, their success either diminishes or they do not enjoy the fruits of their labor.

The Need for Faith in the Self

Failure, to the man or woman who achieves success, can be and often is acutely upsetting, but confidence and a belief in the self ultimately reign supreme. Otherwise, their success would not be sustained.

I treated one man who possessed a severe neurological disturbance but who later emerged as a Ph.D. in the social sciences and wrote several ground-breaking articles for highly regarded journals. When I asked him one day to tell me to what he attributed his ability to overcome failure and achieve success, he replied thoughtfully, "Although my therapy was the catalyst, the answer to your question is that I learned to believe that my strengths belonged to me and that nobody could ever take them away from me."

My patient, Dr. Kaplan, had said something I have never forgotten and have used with many other persons who had difficulty overcoming limitations and failures—our strengths, our capacities, our abilities, our skills are ours forever. Though many can deride us, though many can reject us, though many can deprive us of opportunities, no one can take away our strengths. They are ours to keep forever.

Too many of us incorrectly view our strengths as fleeting possessions, as if one or two rejections can erase them. I have worked in psychotherapy with writers, athletes, and entertainers who needed my help in appreciating what they realistically possessed. I had to show the writers that no matter how many manuscripts were rejected, they had writing skill. For the actors, the dramatic skill was there no matter how many auditions were unsuccessful. And for the athletes, no matter how many strikeouts or fielding errors they committed, their special skills were present even when they were hissed, mocked, and derided. Because sports fans are so ready to become vituperative when a member of their favorite team does not come through with a hit or fails to catch a fly ball, it is crucial for an athlete to believe in his talents. Otherwise, he will hate himself and make more errors until it becomes a self-fulfilling prophecy wherein he warms the bench and becomes the flop he thinks he is. This series of events can happen in many fields of endeavor such as entertainment, the fine arts, or the writing of books.

The successful man or woman, teenager or child, takes the position that failure can be erased but that skills and strengths are permanent possessions. To the successful person, failure is like a mess that can be cleaned up rather than like a bomb that destroys a life.

When failure is accepted, as Neil Simon views it, as a mess to be cleaned up, an insect to be destroyed, it serves as a motivator and can be used to climb the ladder of success. But when failure is experienced as a brutal attack or a severe punishment, instead of climbing the ladder of success we are apt to fall off that ladder and lie prone on the ground, feeling devastated.

In my work I have met many outstanding and potentially outstanding people who have turned their possible success into dismal failures. I saw a graduate of Yale Law School who worked as a clerk in a dime store. I recall an extremely attractive woman, bright and capable, who was on welfare. When I worked with prisoners in jails I encountered many men and women who suffered from deep self-hatred but were extremely capable in one field or another.

What did all these persons have in common? They did not believe they were entitled to success. Usually they hated themselves but did not recognize the depth and pervasiveness of their self-hatred. At times they hated others intensely for reasons they could not fathom. They belittled their talents and gifts and tended to view whatever success they did achieve as a fluke. As we discussed earlier, these people view success as a hostile, destructive triumph in which they injure or destroy others. They are the men and women who were never loved for just being. Often their successes were demeaned by their parents or, as many movie stars and authors and artists feel, they were loved only if they produced.

When successful, such men and women feel they have committed highway robbery, stolen the goodies from either their parents or their siblings, or both. To acknowledge their success to the world is like confessing a crime committed on parents or brothers and sisters. Rather than commit the crime and feel like a criminal, they fail and while destitute and depressed they feel as if they do not have to worry about having destroyed anyone. These persons are in a constant psychological battle, and when they achieve anything they are convinced they have maimed many and destroyed some.

In order to enjoy our successes and keep our failures to a minimum, we have to like ourselves. If as children we were loved for just being, there is a good chance we will not have to defeat ourselves but can enjoy our competencies. Unfortunately, only a small minority in most cultures are really loved for themselves. Most children, as we have pointed out, are loved inconsistently and conditionally, usually because this was the way their parents were treated and their grandparents and great-grandparents. From whom else does the child learn but his parents? A child takes his parent's words and deeds as gospel.

In order to succeed we have to be able to achieve a degree of emotional separation from those who did not and could not appreciate us for just being. We have to follow a Sigmund Freud and say to ourselves, "I like what I think, I like what I do, I like what I've discovered. My mother and father or my siblings may not appreciate who I am or what I do, but they have their limitations, biases and failures to deal with; and I cannot let their voices drown my intelligence."

As Freud once said, "The voice of the intellect is soft but it demands a hearing." In other words, if we have reason to think we have skills and capacities, we should not let the voices of those in the past or present who do not approve of us exert much influence. When we give critical voices too much authority, we are behaving like vulnerable children who want to be loved by those who are unable to truly love us or appreciated by those who do not have the strength or wisdom to appreciate us.

Living with Failure in Order to Succeed

Paradoxically, those who really succeed are those who can live with failure. If failure means the end of the world, if it is viewed as meaning we are despicable, helpless, ugly characters, we will never succeed.

The writer is likely to succeed if he still values his skills and does not experience a rejection of his manuscript as a character assassination. The ballplayer who strikes out, is booed, even ejected from the game by an impatient manager, can become a Neil Simon and return to the ball field if he views the failure realistically. By doing this he is saying that much of his work is permanently good and that to err is human.

Many of us distort failure because we see it as so horrendous, so depleting, so abysmal that we cannot recover from these feelings. A number of academic dropouts at all levels occur in those who can never come in even second best. They must be the best or they are no good at all.

Jackie Mason said, "Being Number One means success and anything less is a failure." It is my belief that he would have enjoyed more triumphs and less poverty at the start if he could have accepted something less than perfection from his performances. It is unfortunate, particularly in American culture, that anything less than Number One is considered by so many as something close to a failure or an actual failure. We can see this on the faces of men and women (actors and actresses) when they are in the same category as the winner of the Academy Awards.

When I coached Little League baseball I often saw many youngsters cry after striking out or after bobbling the ball. Inevitably they were the sons and daughters of parents who yelled and screamed at them for making errors, parents who demanded perfect performance, parents for whom baseball was not for fun.

To succeed at anything requires us to accept as inevitable a failure now and then, at least at the start. Neil Simon failed at the beginning of his career and continues to do so occasionally. Joe Louis and Muhammad Ali both lost fights, as has virtually every world champion. Babe Ruth was well known for striking out, and many later home-run hitters like Daryll Strawberry often strike out, to the boos of spectators. Many a millionaire such as Donald Trump has had to deal with losses, some of them horrendous.

But for all successful people failure is only a temporary state that can be overcome. It is never thought of as permanent because the successful person believes in himself and believes also that he can erase failures. He views achievements as pleasurable, success and notoriety as uplifting, though not ends in themselves.

As the comedian Joey Adams said, "A celebrity works all his life to become famous, then he goes around in dark glasses so nobody will know who he is." Adams realized that becoming a celebrity can be a burden and therefore it is more important to enjoy what we are doing than to seek a notoriety that can create more irritation than joy.

One of the most serious hindrances to leading a pleasurable and productive life is that most of us overrate success. Too often we blame others and ourselves if we have not achieved a great deal of money, fame, and status. Particularly in our society we tend to attribute to those who are rich and famous an ever-present bliss that simply does not exist for any mortal. There are murderous feelings and hatred among the wealthy as well as among the poor.

All too frequently we fail to recognize that multimillionaires are not guaranteed joyous marriages and perfect children. Often we overlook the fact that all-star athletes are subject to deep frustrations and profound depressions, leading many of them to become addicted to alcohol and drugs. History reveals that powerful kings, queens, and emperors have become psychotic, murderous, and suicidal. Men and women with great talents that society esteems highly have destroyed themselves.

Why do we overrate success and ascribe to it such unrealistic attributes? Because when we were children and felt weak and helpless, we assumed that our parents and other adults were omnipotent giants who knew all the answers and lived in consistent happiness. As children we enjoyed playing house, becoming a mommy and daddy, delighted in acting as teacher or doctor, because we felt convinced that adults attained a pleasurable life without one frustration or without one disappointment. If you have ever watched children at play enacting the roles of adults, you will agree that they make themselves appear active, strong, and powerful, totally without vulnerabilities.

The fantasy of Paradise or the Garden of Eden which we all entertain as adults emanates from childhood when we felt that all adults, but particularly our parents, possessed everything while we, the child, had little or nothing.

Tevye, in *Fiddler on the Roof,* assumes that if he were wealthy all of his dreams would come true. Because many of us would like to be athletes, we pay baseball, basketball, and football players millions of dollars a year as we vicariously identify with them when they hit home runs and make difficult catches and interceptions. As we do so, we feel an elation that places us above and beyond the average human being.

Whether a team loses or wins strongly influences our disposition. What do *lose* and *win* mean to us? When we win we feel lovable, desirable to ourselves and to the world. When we lose, we feel despicable, hateful, of no value. The child in us becomes very much alive when we are an adult baseball fan. As our team wins, we feel once again like a loved child.

Just as children cannot accept who they are but wish to be the omnipotent giants their parents appear to them, as adults we continue to nurture the fantasy that those who possess what we do not, reside in an ecstatic state and are to be greatly admired and envied. The grass, we are sure, grows greener on the other side.

Thus we unrealistically believe that one of the best ways to erase failure is to recognize that success, no matter whether it be in business, in academia or in sports, is a cure-all that wipes away all frustration and all disappointments. To the contrary, for us to feel happy, to be productive, to enjoy ourselves and others, we have to diminish the importance of success and truly accept ourselves as we are and others as they are.

Misery—depression, chronic anger, masochism—ensues whenever we chase rainbows that remain in the sky, distant and unapproachable. Life becomes much more enjoyable when we aspire to accomplish what is achievable rather than what is a determined continuation of our childish dreams.

The Perfect Spouse Does not Exist

There would be far fewer divorces and many happier marriages if more of us could accept the fact that *there is no such thing as the perfect spouse*. There would be much more success in the workplace if so many of us did not aspire with such tenacity to be the omnipotent tycoon. Even in our recreations and avocations life would be more fun and more productive if we stayed on earth and monitored more frequently our attempts to climb to the sky and be on top of the world.

I treated a professional golfer who, although extremely talented on the golf course, never placed first in a tournament. His therapy eventually helped him win tournaments after he could emotionally accept the fact that he did not have to achieve holes in one as well as birdies and eagles all the time. As he tried to enjoy himself more, he played golf more competently.

I also recall successfully helping an actress, who had fallen into a deep depression and had constant thoughts about suicide, to accept the fact that she might not be given the leading role in a Broadway production that received rave reviews but could feel happy at being an active participant in a profession she enjoyed. Her peace of mind and her earnings both increased when she modified her burdensome aspirations.

In my work with husbands and wives who have troubled marriages, I have found that they start to feel happier and function better when they demand less of each other and less of themselves.

Mabel and Jack, a married couple in their late twenties, arrived at my office for what they called divorce counseling. Each was deeply dissatisfied with the other. Mabel wanted more intellectual stimulation, and Jack wanted more sexual stimulation from his wife. Mabel asked for more help from Jack in her work as a public relations director, and Jack, insisting on privacy with regard to his work, said he wanted Mabel "to mind her own business more and leave me alone."

As I listened to Mabel and Jack, I thought of the dozens of married couples I had worked with who had brought similar complaints. They all demanded more from their partners and felt very deprived and deeply misunderstood. Slowly Jack and Mabel, like the other couples I have counseled, started to enjoy each other and themselves when they learned to accept one another *as they were* rather than *as they wished them to be.*

Most unhappy marriages exist because husband and wife cannot accept the fact that, like all human relationships, marriage has its limitations, frustrations, and disillusionments.

But marriages do not have to be unfulfilling if the partners realize it was not designed to or never will solve frustrations and problems existing since childhood. The sad fact is that almost everyone expects marriage will miraculously erase the earlier pains and aches that still persist and will continue to persist if its origins are not faced.

The Need to Redefine Success

One of the clear misconceptions in our society holds that there is a direct relationship between fame and happiness. In the early 1990s an editorial in the *New York Times* asked, "What do these great writers have in common—Tolstoi, Ibsen, Proust, Joyce and Strindberg?"

The answer to this question was that none of the men was deemed worthy of the Nobel Prize in Literature. All these famous writers continued being creative and productive even though they did not receive the most prestigious of literary awards. They may have felt momentarily hurt, but they did not allow their sorrow or anger to stand in the way of producing further magnificent books.

Too many of us tend to believe that the value of our work, whether it be in the office or at home, should be judged on the basis of the accolades we receive. Yet it is clear to a good many observers that some who have received accolades like the Nobel prizes have not been the most creative and productive of writers. This probably holds true of awards in other fields, including politics, the fine arts, and the sciences.

Yet we all continue to seek accolades and to judge ourselves by the number we receive, as well as to judge others by the number they receive. What causes this persistent and intense desire for recognition and approval?

The answer lies in our powerful wish to recapture over and over again the delightful, wonderful feeling of childhood when our mother, father, grandparent, or teacher said to us, "You've done marvelously. You're the best—and I love you!" Such words, sadly enough, told us we were loved perhaps especially because we had done marvelously, were the best.

We would all be much more successful if we were not so eager to receive applause and recognition daily. When we feel angry about the applause we do not receive or the recognition that does not come our way, we should remind ourselves that we are reenacting the role of a little child who needs parental sustenance in order to like ourselves, to feel we are "somebody important."

As we have pointed out throughout this book, the child within remains with us a lifetime, wanting to be loved and adored, gratified and indulged. The vital question really is: "How can I talk to and deal with this child inside me?"

First we must realize that it is natural for the child to wish to be the most loved and adored person in the world, the "biggest and the best." We have to accept that it is natural for the child in us to feel, "I am angry when I do not get the love and approval for which I yearn."

If a child did not receive a certain amount of love and

attention from caring parents, as often occurs, he will demand from others even more stridently what he did not receive from his parents.

After the child in us is allowed to speak to the adult within and express his needs and wishes, his disappointments and his anger, we may then assure ourselves we are adults who should no longer seek the eternal breast or the eternal orgasm. If we give the child in us time to express himself, his yearnings, and unfulfilled desires, we are far more able to accept with greater equanimity the adult in ourselves. We can then face the realities we must endure as an adult, realities that we have not yet confronted maturely because we have been too much influenced by the angry child within.

To erase failure and enjoy success, we need to redefine success. Instead of equating it with fame, glory, and notoriety, we might better define success as the ability to love, to empathize with others, and to like ourselves *as we are.*

Failure, then, is hating others and hating ourselves. We have failed if we find ourselves degrading others and demeaning ourselves as we overidealize success and equate it with fame and fortune. True success emanates from liking ourselves and others without asking for glory.

A good example of this kind of success was described by John MacLeod, when he was coach of the New York Knickerbockers basketball team. His philosophy in coaching basketball players is to help each player learn how to cooperate with his teammates. MacLeod said on television during a practice session of his team, "If you make somebody else on the team feel good, you start to feel good. Then with both of you feeling good, your energy is available to win the game. You're a much better player when you love your teammates."

The more we love and the less we hate, the more we will achieve and the more we will enjoy just being alive. First, we have to try to be aware of our hatred, then understand that most hatred which persists in adulthood is a product of unrealistic, childish wishes. We hate when we have not received the equivalent of parental adulation. We hate when we cannot accept frustration as part of everyday living. We hate when we insist on being loved all the time—a most unrealistic demand that leads to disaster.

Most people who continue to hate into adulthood are carrying on a futile battle with their parents and others who were not able to love them. This futile battle is the most pernicious verbal poison devised by mankind, most responsible in creating a sense of failure.

If we cannot say to ourselves, "My mother or father, sister or brother, teacher or grandmother had their serious limitations, perhaps even their emotional illnesses, and that's the way it was," we will continue to hate and to fail. We will be unable to love anyone because we do not love ourselves.

But when we can love, we feel far more pleasure in our life. We become more creative, more energetic, more compassionate. One female patient, a writer, told me, after several years of treatment, "I find myself now able to write three books a year instead of one. I know it's because I feel I am far more at peace with myself, my parents, and my siblings. I no longer have to deny or hold back childhood feelings of despair and hatred."

Part of loving and therefore being successful lies in recognizing that to be human means to be imperfect, vulnerable, and prone to make mistakes. When we can accept the imperfections in ourselves and others, life becomes much more enjoyable.

In the book *Once More Around the Park* Roger Angell

talks poignantly about the joys inherent in being an imperfect human being. Commenting on the difference between a raucous early-1960s Mets fan, watching his team lose yet another time at Shea Stadium, and a dignified Yankee fan watching his team at the Yankee Stadium, Angell writes:

> This was a new recognition that perfection is admirable but a trifle inhuman, and that a stumbling kind of semi-success can be much more warming. Most of all, perhaps, these exultant yells for the Mets were also yells for ourselves, and came from a wry, half-understood recognition that there is more Met than Yankee in every one of us. I knew for whom that foghorn blew; it blew for me.

In reviewing this book for the *New York Times*, March 16, 1991, Herbert Mitgang, who seems to understand baseball as well as he does success and failure, describes it as "a baseball book for all seasons." He goes on:

> It's written so gracefully that the temptation is to treat this selection of his memorable pieces, written by an unabashed lover of the game who has covered 29 World Series for *The New Yorker*, only as literature. That would count as an error. For the most learned fan is bound to discover nuances about the game, unnoticed until the author reported and interpreted them.

Mitgang concludes:

> What puts *Once More Around the Park* on the big-league shelf is, above all, language and, after that, respect for the individuality and awe for the profes-

> sionalism of its characters. Mr. Angell makes baseball sound like an art form; he demonstrates that writing about it is an art form, too.

Perhaps what Angell said about the pleasure involved in being a Mets fan in the 1960s could be used by those who coach and counsel Little Leaguers and other children and teenagers, so that from the start they enjoy the game. If the emphasis were placed on fun, love, and cooperation, Little League baseball could be a much more maturing experience for youngsters than it often is.

Our redefinition of success would involve modifications in many institutions of our society. We would have to emphasize much more than we have that children, in order to love and to function well as adults, need two loving parents who understand each other and themselves and who enjoy cooperating in the enhancement of the life of their child.

Education, the workplace, and many other institutions in our society would need to emphasize the importance of human happiness as the top priority rather than tangible productivity. As Amy Saltzman in her book *Down-Shifting* points out, a growing number of American men and women are enjoying life more as they spend less time and energy trying to be famous and concentrate more on giving their family members and themselves more pleasure and comfort.

In his book *Mothers, Leadership and Success,* Guy Odom points out that success is no accident. He discovered that children of parents who are dominant and successful often become underachievers. He details some of the consequences of child neglect and child abuse, finding that when parents cannot love, they produce unlovable children.

Although dramatic changes in society are needed to ensure happier and more productive adults and children, all of us can erase much failure and enjoy more success in our current society as we continue to cope with the many limitations imposed on us by our neurotic culture.

CHAPTER 11

TEN STEPS TO THE TOP OF THE LADDER OF SUCCESS

The following ten steps may help many unhappy men and women move toward a much more enjoyable life, a much more productive life, and a much more loving life:

1. Accept the Fact That You Can Be Successful!

In order to be successful at anything—work, love, parenting, study, or sports—you have to believe that you have the right to be successful. Too much of the time you feel like a guilty child in a world of huge adults, contending that to succeed is like trespassing on forbidden territory.

But you do have the right to an enjoyable love life, providing you do not look at yourself as a naughty child in bed with a parental figure. You do have the right to succeed at work, providing you do not view your competitive and ambitious wishes as reasons for punishment. You can communicate easily if you give yourself the right to talk as an assertive adult.

If you grant yourself the right to feel the respect and love of others—family and friends—you will start to receive respect and love. Extend to yourself the right to enjoy a decent life and you will possess one. Remember: If you think you are beaten you are. If you think you dare not, you don't. If you think you would like to win but believe you cannot, it's almost a cinch you won't.

2. *Set Yourself Realistic Goals!*

To be a winner you have to be realistic about what you can and cannot attain. Most of us either overestimate or underrate our capacities. Sometimes we make ourselves too large in our minds, other times too small. Few of us heed Socrates' admonition: "Know thyself." To know yourself means to be very clear about what you can and what you cannot do.

Most of us have the capacity to love and be loved, to work productively, and to relax in pleasure. We should exercise these capacities and derive the gratification from them that is rightfully ours. However, most of us are not Einsteins, Freuds, or Babe Ruths and we should try to accept our human limitations and curb our fantasies of omnipotence. The more human we permit ourselves to be, the more we will succeed.

To really know ourselves better we often have to consult friends, family members, and colleagues to acquire some consensual validation regarding our talents and skills. Occasionally we have to consult experts and take aptitude tests to learn about our real skills and true strengths. Once we know ourselves better, the next job is to get started without too much wavering and move toward the realization of our goals—whether the goal is a new job, a new lover, a course in a university, a new hobby, or a loss of weight.

3. You Cannot Succeed All at Once—It Has to Be One Step at a Time!

All too often you have failed because you have wanted too much too soon. Rome was not built in a day, and a truly successful person was not created in a day. Too many of us do not set wise plans for ourselves, nor do we calculate the necessary steps to reach our destiny, as we would if we were to take a motor trip from New York to Los Angeles.

The prudent traveler plans in advance and sets realistic goals for each day. So, too, when we plan to make a business venture successful or when we try to master a new skill such as deep-sea diving, or win an election in a political campaign, we have to plan our activities in advance, give ourselves realistic time limits and see how one step ahead can lead to another. If you are interested in getting involved in a love affair, you have to know the kind of person you really want, where and whether you can find the person you have in mind, how you will spend your time with the prospective lover, how you will evaluate progress, what inhibitions you will have to overcome, and what possible compromises you are willing to make.

One of the main issues in succeeding at a project is to plan your activities in advance, setting up realistic and attainable goals and knowing how you are going to accomplish each step along the way.

4. Give Yourself Rewards—We All Need Reinforcements!

Few of us can accomplish any task without some kind of approval, recognition, or reward. Sometimes we can reward ourselves, as when we allow ourselves to take an afternoon nap after mowing a lawn, go on a vacation following an arduous work project, or buy a dress or suit after losing weight. Sometimes persons we feel close to will be happy to listen to us brag about our accomplishments, then pat us on the back. If we know who our supporters are, we should feel free to enlist their warmth and encouragement when we feel lonely and isolated.

We all have our own reward system. Some of us feel reinforced by a compliment; others detest this form of enhancement. Some of us are enriched by a purchase we would not usually make; others are turned off by this act.

Find some way to give yourself encouragement and support. Find others to reward you in ways that are comfortable to you.

5. Failure Is Inevitable Along the Way in Almost Everything You Undertake! Accept It as a Given!

You have to accept some losses in order to win, accept some failures in order to succeed. If you do not berate yourself endlessly for failing at something or if you do not vent your spleen for days and weeks after you have not achieved what you want, you are on the road to success.

Too often you have reacted to frustration and failure as if you were a prince or a princess and had temper tantrums when you did not get what you wanted. You cannot command success—you have to work hard for it. When things do not go your way (and from time to time they won't) don't consider the failure as meaning that the end of your world has arrived and your demise is near.

Consider failure for what it truly is—a realistic disappointment which gives you the right to feel indignant, though not forever. If you are busy fuming and fretting, or if you are constantly angry at others, you are compounding your failures and delaying success.

Most of us are capable of much more success in those activities in which we are involved, but too many of us cannot risk failure. We feel humiliated by it, as if we were a cast-off child with severe physical and mental handicaps rather than a human mortal who has real strengths and real limitations. If we do not distort the meaning of failure, it can do for us what it has done for a Neil Simon—push us back to work.

6. Do Not Overrate Success!

You are never going to be the omnipotent giant you want to be—loved and admired by all, blessed with valuable possessions and enormous power, able to win friends and influence people all of the time. Bliss is momentary and ecstasy transient. If you are looking for permanent peace you will have to wait until you are dead. If you are looking for permanent ecstasy, you would have to return to your mother's breast, which is impossible.

To be successful in what you want to succeed at—love, work, study, hobbies—you have to keep reminding yourself that if you achieve your ambitions, though your self-esteem will rise, your self-confidence will grow, and your relationships with others will improve, you can never bank on becoming a multimillionaire, the writer of best-sellers, or a stage or screen star who is loved and applauded twenty-four hours a day, seven days a week.

The psychiatrist Dr. Harry Stack Sullivan wrote: "We are all more human than otherwise." We can be much more successful if we lessen our arrogance, diminish our competitive spirit, and accept the fact that regardless of our attainment, religion, gender, or color, we are all pretty much the same.

7. Take Responsibility for Your Mature and Immature Actions!

Succeeding requires a strong sense of responsibility. If we get good results in whatever we have undertaken, we should be aware of what we have actually done that helped us accomplish our goals. If we have not achieved what we believe is achievable, we should reassess how realistic our goals have been and whether we really do have the capacities to attain what we desire.

If we have not succeeded but do have the capacities and skills to accomplish realistic goals, then we have to ask ourselves where we went wrong. For example, if the business is not making a profit, the state of the economy might be a factor. But did we overlook something? Did we hire the wrong person? invest in the wrong items? settle in the wrong locations? fight too much with others?

Most failures in work, love, and elsewhere are caused by an unwillingness to take responsibility for our own provocations, oversights, or insensitivities. Wives blame husbands and husbands blame wives when marriages are riddled with conflict. Neither accepts sufficient responsibility, and the marriage remains a field of battle. The same is true of relations between management and labor, teachers and students, parents and children. When there is conflict, the parties involved are not facing themselves and each other honestly.

Successful relationships require both parties to take responsibility for their own mistakes, to empathize with each other, and to demonstrate some flexibility. Relationships that end in failure occur when the individuals involved constantly blame each other for their frustrations, demand indulgence, and are unforgiving when slighted.

8. Realize That Feeling Depressed and Sorry for Yourself Is a Coward's Way Out!

Nobody likes to be disappointed. No one finds frustration, rejection, or unkindness easy to take. All of us prefer to be treated fairly, kindly, lovingly, and compassionately. Particularly when we work hard, care for others, and make sacrifices, we would like to be given some consideration by others.

Unfortunately, we live in an imperfect world which at times is very unfair to the decent people that most of us are. This is one of the most painful realities of life to accept—that others violate the Golden Rule and often do not treat us as well as we treat them. But this is the way life is at times.

What will be debilitating and destructive for you is to nurture disappointment and constantly collect injustices. To feel sorry for yourself and remind others and yourself how you have been mistreated only weakens you, lowers your self-esteem and makes others resent you. To accept the fact that a feeling of disappointment and frustration in marriage, work, and elsewhere is par for the course is a large step toward success. To fume and fuss keeps you a nagging child, which is cowardly and gets you nowhere.

The hallmarks of feeling more positive about the self include: You have learned to forgive your parents for what they may have done early in your life to distress you emotionally; you have learned to say no and all that implies—you are now friendly with your own principles and ideals and can tolerate the resentment of others because you approve more highly of yourself; you have learned to say yes without feeling crushed or demeaned. You have become more creative and more competent.

9. Do Not Be Afraid to Ask for Help!

Too many people lack the courage to ask for help. They fail to realize that it takes strength to admit that they are not and never will be omnipotent, independent giants. They do not understand that those who cannot ask others for support, understanding, or direction are hiding something from themselves. What they hide is a sense of enormous fragility and vulnerability.

They distort the act of being helped and interpret it as meaning that they appear to be helpless children when they are supported. To deny feeling helpless they act like powerful robots, fooling themselves but feeling depressed and miserable anyway.

No man or woman is an island. Whether we acknowledge it or not, all human beings need other human beings to feel worthwhile. We have to remind ourselves that we are not clinging vines or pesky children when we ask for a friendly ear, a pat on the back, or a piece of advice. Those who succeed are those who have not felt humiliated by asking for help.

10. Like Yourself!

Any man, woman, or child who is successful at anything has had to like himself or herself while doing what he or she is seeking to accomplish. If we hate ourselves for our ambitions, we will have to sabotage them one way or another.

Those who fail in love relationships do not like themselves as they try to give and receive pleasure. They feel either guilty or unworthy. Nobody deserves to be deprived of love, so don't work hard withholding it from yourself or from others. Take love from others, return it, and also give it to yourself.

To work productively, to enjoy a sexual life, to possess a self-respecting role in a family and in the community, we have to like ourselves as we go about satisfying ourselves and others. When we are not liking ourselves we have to find out why. Most often we will realize that we are punishing ourselves for thoughts and fantasies that hurt no one. When we have actually hurt others, we are entitled to forgive ourselves after we understand how and why we acted erroneously.

It may take time to change our state of mind if we feel depressed and unhappy, but if we explore our feelings and how they relate to behavior we will find that our need to punish the self gradually lessens, then disappears.

We will also discover as we explore in depth what has troubled us over the years how we have dramatized and overestimated our early fears and hatreds. To bring this to awareness is the best medicine that we can administer to ourselves. We can then live without fear of failure and judge success in terms of enjoying every day for whatever it offers. We know at last it is the way we think of ourselves, like ourselves, and feel comfortable with ourselves, free of the past early torments, that determines our inner sense of freedom and happiness.

In the early 1900s Dr. Karen Horney, a noted psychoanalyst, said, "Fortunately, psychoanalysis is not the only way to resolve inner conflicts. Life itself still remains a very effective therapist." Yes, life can be an effective therapist, but we also have to administer the taste of therapy ourselves at times if we want to enjoy life without feeling driven, desperate, or uneasy. This each of us can achieve if we do what Socrates advised: "Know thyself." Know the child within us as well as the adult we have become and we will live far more happily.